It Takes All Kinds

Books by Lloyd Lewis

SHERMAN: FIGHTING PROPHET

MYTHS AFTER LINCOLN

CHICAGO: A HISTORY OF ITS REPUTATION
(*with Henry Justin Smith*)

IT TAKES ALL KINDS

LLOYD LEWIS

It Takes All Kinds

New York

HARCOURT, BRACE AND COMPANY

Contents

Author's Note	ix
OLD TOM'S CABINS	3
HE HATED SOUTHERN GENTLEMEN	13
THE SECRET EVANGEL OF OTTO MC FEELY	31
THAT COLD, HARD EYE	35
MY BIGGEST BASEBALL DAY	39
THE BATTLE OF KILPATRICK'S PANTS	47
A DREAMLIKE CONCERN	67
LAST OF THE TROUBADOURS	73
THE HOLY SPIRIT AT WEST POINT	82
BILLY THE KID	101
THE RATS AND CATS AT TERRE HAUTE	120
A HYMN FROM AN ABATTOIR	123
THE OLD JUDGE	142
THE HILL CALLED CROWDER'S CURSE	145
THE MAN THE HISTORIANS FORGOT	149
"KEEP MOVIN'"	177
"DE LAWD'S" ONLY FRIEND	185
THEY DIDN'T WANT "FREE ENTERPRISE"	188
NOT IN "THE GREEN PASTURES"	192
KING OF THE BULL PEN	196
THEY ARE WRONG ABOUT WRIGHT	200

HEAVE-HO, SILVER!   204

THE GREAT WINNETKA HUNT   208

REFORM IS WHERE YOU FIND IT   211

A FOUNDING FATHER RETURNS   215

THE BIG SHOULDERS SAG   219

ORCHIDS TO MRS. EINSTEIN   223

WOOLLCOTT, HORNER & WHITE   226

LIFE WITH UNCLE EGGS   230

BACKWOODS ARISTOCRAT   238

"SEND OFF, AND GET LOTS OF MAIL"   242

BEYOND FLESH AND BLOOD   247

DOUBLE MARTYRDOM FOR LINCOLN   251

"THE GLORY-TO-GOD MAN"   254

Sources   275

Author's Note

THAT it takes all kinds of people to make a world is a cliché which any reporter should never use in his writing, yet it states a fact which he should be the first to extol. If it were actually anything less than a cliché, he would be living in a world so packed with stock characters and standardized types that he would be reduced to writing editorials about international drifts or essays on national trends.

If a reporter will look back upon what he has written across the years, he can see, just as I have been seeing, that the pieces which now interest him most are those which report not what he himself thought and did, but what other people thought, said, and did.

In some of the pieces I have written for newspapers, magazines, or historical publications—pieces about personalities in sport, literature, sheep-ranching, the theater, the Civil War, or the general life of a large city—I can recapture the varying emotions, the excitement, the amusement, the anger, or the sorrow I felt at the time I made the report.

Only such articles as these have been included in this book, and if any reader should now share those emotions it would be grateful news, indeed, since what a reporter really wants is not to get himself in between the personality he is writing about and the person he is writing to.

Libertyville, Ill.   LLOYD LEWIS

It Takes All Kinds

Old Tom's Cabins

LIVING alone in a log cabin on the western slope of the Rockies in northwestern Colorado was no hardship for Old Tom Blevins. He was of Irish blood, and instead of entertaining himself with tales of the pixies and banshees he made up stories about the world today—the world he sensed from stray newspapers or from occasional talks with ranchers or hunters who rode by.

Jay Monaghan, who was a sheep baron then—long before he came back East to become the Lincoln author that he is—Monaghan grubstaked Old Tom just to hear those stories. It was worth a long pack trip from Jensen, Utah, on the State line, up through the desert and across the mountains into Pat's Hole and the scrub-cedar wilderness just to hear Tom talk.

When I would be there, Monaghan and I would sit for hours in the old man's cabin listening to his flights of imagination. It was true, we supposed, that he had in the 1870's thrown down his brickmason's trowel, as he said he had, and quit Evansville, Indiana, for the excitements of punching cows in Texas. But we were never sure he had actually had all the adventures he said he'd had with William Bonner, otherwise known as Billy the Kid.

My, he'd say, how Billy had admired him—admired the way he could go straight and keep out of trouble while Billy had gone to the bad. Billy had got killed while

Tom had gone on to enjoy a wonderful life. Tom would tell all about the exploits and death of Billy the Kid—and tell it better than anybody either Monaghan and I had ever heard; he'd tell about the time he was Tom Blevins, the Locomotive Engineer, on the train that took Coxey's Army to Washington.

"We got there," said Tom, "and marched around the White House and saw old Grover Cleveland lookin' out the window and laughin' at us. That was about the time Old Grover kicked his wife down the White House steps."

If Tom imagined someone had injured him, he was not above touching up his tale with a few flicks of kindly libel. And when he had got off a lie like this about the domestic affairs of the Clevelands, he would stroke his long mustachios and smile to himself.

One of his more romantic legends had to do with the time he had guided Jay Gould over the choice portions of Texas, when that railroad emperor wanted to survey the possibilities of the Southwest. Tom said he had ridden with Jay Gould and Jay's young daughter, Helen, on the special car for days, till Jay suddenly dispensed with his services. Tom hinted that Jay Gould had found no fault with his running fire of information on the resources of Texas, but what had moved the rich old fellow was the discovery that Helen was becoming too interested in their guide.

Tom's wildest concoction was the story that he had seen Oscar Wilde hiding out in Texas, "sometime after he got into that trouble with Prince Albert." Oscar was well disguised, but he couldn't fool Old Tom.

"I didn't turn him in, though," Blevins would say with a virtuous smirk.

Tom's fantasies played upon the modern scene, as well. He had tales of President Coolidge's vast silences. "They say he's dumb," Tom would observe, then after a sage pause would add, "He looks deaf, too."

Tom would walk around his dusty, disheveled cabin, hanging hams on nails beside defunct saddles while he re-created for us the Homeric prize fight between two characters whom he called Dumpsey and Flippo. He had made practically a saga out of a politico-economic war between President Winslow and an engineer named Hoov-over in which the entire Railroad Board had narrowly escaped hanging.

While he wove these enchantments, embroidered with mispronunciations and reckless misconstructions, he would cook, wipe the dishes on a soiled grain sack, then throw the dishwater on the dirt floor of his cabin, observing, in explanation, "Hardens it."

Neither Monaghan nor I ever slept inside Tom's cabin at night, preferring to roll up in blankets outside under the spruce trees. The sheets on Old Tom's bed were as brown as the blankets, and the ancient cowhand was understood to make this bed twice a year—once in the springtime and once in the fall. We never saw him do more in the way of cleansing himself than dip the tips of his fingers in a bucket of spring water and dampen the very top of his brow. Nobody would be coming to see him. Why fix up? Monaghan and I—that was different; we brought him his food. He repaid us, he fully believed, with sagacious advice on how to handle sheep and how to outguess the cattlemen of Colorado who were, at the time, quite emphatic in ordering all sheepmen back across the deadline into Utah.

Many and stirring were the stories told us of these long-lived stock wars, and some of his descriptions of Tom Horn, the stock detective of the region who had been hanged over in Denver, Monaghan later used in his history of Horn, *The Last of the Bad Men*.

The fewer people Tom saw, the more freely his imagination could roam. He didn't hanker for society. Of the sheep herders who occasionally dropped in to eat with him, he'd say, "They're bad cooks. Why, their sons-a-bitchen biscuits are harder'n the back of God's head."

What he liked to eat were prunes and pancakes. He would eat the bacon and the hams we would bring in to him twice a year, along with six months' supply of flour, buckwheat, syrup, salt, sugar, lard, and staples of that kind, but he didn't feel quite right about eating meat, for he did want to be a Pythagorean. Living there in the heart of one of the best of the big game countries, he refused to take life. The deer would trample the scrawling little garden he pretended to cultivate, but Old Tom would never shoot them. His big mongrel hound, Keno, would chase jack rabbits right up to the door, but Old Tom would never take down the rifle which had hung, unused, twenty years or more. His other dog, Friskie, was a white poodle who practically never went out of the cabin. Tom had quite a story about how he came by Friskie. It boiled down to, "Friskie was give me by that big, fat chippie who used to stay in the town of Red Onion. Can't recall her name; we all just knew her as 'The Covered Wagon.'"

Usually Old Tom had another pet—a cat named Old Mitts. If the cat died, he got another as soon as he could and called it Old Mitts, too. He said he always had one because he liked the way that first Old Mitts had behaved the time his wife left him.

Tom had got his wife through "The Heart and Hand" column in the *Denver Post* and, as he told it, had given her, on their wedding night, instructions as to what he expected.

"I wound that alarm clock, there," he told us, pointing to a long-dead timepiece on the log shelf, "set it fer six, and, as we climbed into bed, I told her, 'Now when that rings, I want to hear your feet flap on the floor.'"

After three months Tom's wife left him: "Said she was going into Jensen to get some things, and I saddled up Old Cody and she rode off down through that draw. It was spring and the fireweed was over the hills. She waved as she went out of sight behind that rock, and I waved and turned around to go back into the house and there in the door stood Old Mitts, wavin' her tail goodbye, too."

Mrs. Blevins never came back, though she left his horse, properly enough, at the feedbarn with the note which explained her reasons for departing. Tom never revealed to us what the note contained. He kept her wedding clothes in a grain sack and every so often would take them out to burn, but would wind up cursing softly and stuffing them back in the bag again.

It must have been the sixth or seventh cat in that succession of Old Mitts which produced a temporary revolution in Blevins' soul. Monaghan learned about it one November when he rode in with Tom's winter supply of grub. The old man started goddamming before he could ask Monaghan to come in or how he was or how long he could stay.

"God damn 'em," he snorted. "God damn them coyotes; they've et Old Mitts. She's been gone a week now, and I've sent to town fer twenty steel traps and three dollars' worth of poison and 200 cartridges. I've oiled up the rifle, and I'm going to spend the winter killin' coyotes. They'll pay fer this."

He could talk of nothing else all that evening and next day and it was amid his profane volleys of promised revenges that Monaghan rode away to be gone till spring would let him come up through the mountain passes again.

When Monaghan did come back the next March, he halted the pack train as he neared the cabin. What had happened? The cabin looked like a carnival tent, with banners or something fluttering along its walls. He rode nearer and saw that the cabin was covered with coyote hides, their fur moving in the spring wind.

Monaghan shouted, and out came Old Tom looking as if he had been killing sheep.

"I guess I made a kind of a fool of myself, Jimmy," he said. (He always called Monaghan, "Jimmy.") "You remember when you left last fall I told you I was goin' to get even with them coyotes? Well, there they are, forty-five of 'em. I shot and trapped all winter—froze one foot, lost old Keno, lamed my horse, but I got 'em."

Monaghan said Tom looked at the trophies bashfully, scratched his bottom shyly, then added, "Well, day before yesterday that chinook struck and the snow melted and I said, 'I guess spring's here so I think I'll make my bed.' I carried it out here into the yard and give it a shake and out fell Old Mitts, pressed as pretty as a flower."

A few months after that, Monaghan found an excuse

to move Tom out of his castle of squalor and into a fresh cabin. He explained to Old Tom that he had to have somebody watch a gate over at Cockleburr Springs, about twenty miles across the mountains. Cockleburr was one of the few fenced-in areas on Monaghan's sheep-range— a 200-acre oasis of thin grass amid a barren expanse of rocks. It was where the ewes, in their migratory driftings, stopped to drop their lambs in the spring as they passed from the winter range of the Utah deserts to the green summer range on top of the Rockies. Although there was little enough of this grass, sufficient grew around some little springs to feed the ewes during their confinement.

Monaghan moved Tom over and explained the situation, "Now all you've got to do is to keep that gate closed so the wild horses and deer and burros won't eat up what grass there is. Just watch that gate! This cabin won't be home to you, Tom, but it's got a good roof and is nearer civilization. That road down there can be used by automobiles if they go slow, and I can get in to you oftener with grub. It'll be fresher."

Tom professed to like the change, although the scenery was a comedown. From the cabin you looked out across the skimpy little pool of green grass to a huge, dry, bleak, rocky desert. It was where the timber-covered Rockies smoothed out into the big desert that runs clear across Utah—an expanse populated with a few small ranchers and, just over in Utah, by the Ute Indians on their reservation.

Old Tom had been at Cockleburr Springs for five or six months when I arrived on a visit, and as Monaghan drove me along the dirt road, he said that Old Tom was sure anxious to see me—needed my help in starting a new business.

"It seems," said Monaghan, "that Tom's decided those little fool springs that seep out around the cabin are highly medicinal. You remember how he came from southern Indiana, and I suppose he is thinking about French Lick and West Baden. Anyway, he wants you and me to finance him in turning Cockleburr into a health resort. Play up to him, will you?"

I said I would, and when we landed at Tom's cabin and he asked me how I was, I delighted him by saying I had a bad touch of sciatica.

"Right over here," he crowed, and led me to a mudhole he had shoveled out around one of the little seepages. "Git in there. It's just the ticket fer sciatica."

I peeled down and, by lying flat, could almost immerse myself in the tepid water. And as I lay there he squatted on his heels and gave me his vision of the dream-spa. Several marble bathhouses would stand where we were. Just across that arroyo would be the main hotel. The cottages would be up the hill, there. All it would take to clear the ground would be a couple of trucks of dynamite. Down in the treeless, baking valley would rise the gambling casino. At the gate a big electric sign would throw the spa's name a hundred miles across the desert.

The old man's hands trembled as they swept back and forth across that God-forsaken landscape, and I began to feel like a hypocrite. But I was in for it, so I told him, when he interrupted his discourse to inquire about my sciatica, "She's quittin' me, Tom. I can feel her go. Another treatment, tomorrow, will fix her for good."

"I knew it; I knew it," he kept saying as he led the

way, walking like a boy on those high-heeled boots of his, over to his cabin and supper. All that evening he macadamized the road for fifty miles each way, backed railroad presidents into corners and forced them to put in spurs to handle the transcontinental crowds, and, as I recall it, he was building a golf course when we bedded down for the night.

It was like this for two days, then Monaghan and I had to go to see about some grazing rights, and as we left I told Tom I'd sure see what could be done about the money in Chicago. I didn't like to lie to him, but Monaghan had kept insisting, "Stick in there. Your visit will give him entertainment for a whole year, chewing this over. He'll get down to business now, after you leave, and do some real things with that imagination of his."

Tom stood by the car as we started, saying, "There's millions in it fer all three of us."

I had been back in Chicago two weeks when a letter came from Monaghan saying that he had driven to Cockleburr to see Tom and had arrived to find the gate open—standing wide open—and Tom gone.

"I saw by the horse tracks that he had ridden out the day before," the letter ran, "and had turned down the valley between the Great Hogback and Dead Man's Bench. I shut the gate and followed the tracks till they turned off a little later into the hills. I kept going on the road, and, after about fifteen minutes, I suddenly made out somebody riding, hell for leather, up near the top of the Hogback, heading back toward Cockleburr. I stopped the car and waited and soon saw it was Old Tom. I honked the horn, he heard, and turned his horse down to the road. When he came up, I asked him what was wrong. He'd left the gate open.

"His jaw dropped. He said, God, he was sorry about that. He was sure he had shut it tight. This was terrible. He said he'd run out of tobacco yesterday afternoon and had ridden down to borrow some from his nearest neighbor, a sheep herder twelve miles down the valley.

"He said, 'I was there with that herder in the tent when Marcus Jenson (a rancher some fifteen miles the other side of Cockleburr) rode up and got off his horse and said he'd come a-past the Spa and happened to mention that he'd seen two old Ute Indians a-settin' in the spring. So I saddled up quick. I've gotta get back there, because, Jesus Christ, Jimmy, we're gittin' the wrong class of people!' "

He Hated Southern Gentlemen

THE first of December, 1851, was a dark day for Southern fire-eaters, although none of them apparently realized it at the time. To all appearances the weather in their brightest heaven, the United States Senate, was still calm and fair as they set about organizing that body in what had come to be the traditional Southern manner. But in reality two clouds had come up over the horizon—clouds that for all their apparent lightness were packed with storm and thunder.

Two new senators walked to the front and took the oath of office—two Northerners, fit only for the polite contempt of Southern gentlemen who had been born to rule the chamber. One, a forty-year-old Apollo, answering to the name of Charles Sumner, appeared to be too intent upon his pompadour ever fully to fill those shoes of Daniel Webster into which he was stepping. The other, Benjamin Franklin Wade, just an old judge from Ohio, was even less impressive as he stood there, heavy, glum, and square, lifting a right hand that had been flattened by ax- and shovel-handles. A self-made, untutored yokel, he was whispered to be, and innocent enough to have brought his squirrel-rifle with him to Washington.

Further than to assign the newcomers to the tail-ends of minor committees, the fire-eaters paid them no heed, which, although an error, was quite natural. Southern gentlemen had been ruling the Senate since the first days

of the Republic, and they felt it to be their hereditary
Olympus, upon which Northerners and Westerners must
be always ill at ease and more or less apologetic. Pointed
from infancy toward statecraft, the aristocratic scions of
the Cotton Kingdom believed senatorial togas to be their
hereditary costume and the Senate Chamber the predes-
tined theater of their performance. In the House of Representatives, the home of commoner men, presumptuous
and vulgar Yankees, such as Thad Stevens and Joshua
Giddings, might criticize and even denounce the Slave
Power, but nothing so *gauche* could happen in the Senate.
There even, the best of Northern and Western leaders—
even Webster, Douglas, and Clay—had come, in the end,
to admit the Cavalier supremacy. At any rate, they had
acted so, scurrying to fix up compromises that would
wheedle the fire-eaters from walking out of the Union.
The Supreme Court, too, obeyed the South. As for the
Presidency, hadn't it been held by one Southern man or
another for forty out of its sixty-two years?

No, there seemed no cause for worry in 1851, even if
John C. Calhoun, king of the Southern spokesmen, had
been a year in his grave. In his seat was Robert B. Rhett,
South Carolina's chief baiter of Northern Abolitionists
and editor of the Charleston *Mercury*, the principal organ
of the proslavery extremists; Jefferson Davis was there
from Mississippi, as was Henry S. Foote, who had fought
Benton of Missouri a splendid fist-fight on the floor of
the Senate. All these men were Southerners first, Whigs
or Democrats afterwards. Some of them were amiable,
tolerant; more of them were fire-eaters. All were intent
upon teaching the North to keep its grubby hands off the
divine institution of slavery.

To match them the opposition had nobody. Webster had left to become Secretary of State. Clay, the Kentucky Unionist, was there in his seat for no more than the opening day, a toothless tiger now, seventy-four years old, a mere six months of life left in him. Stephen A. Douglas, of Illinois, was buzzing around, tickling the slave-owners with a feather, dreaming of the Presidency. Douglas was no menace to the aristocrats. He might have ability, but Senator Thomas Hart Benton of Missouri had polished him off one day while watching the Little Giant go down the street. "No, sir!" mused Benton loudly. "He'll never be President. The seat of his pants is too close to the ground!"

Indeed, the entire North had the seat of its pants very near to the dust in 1851. The Southern breathers of flame ran over the Yankee senators mercilessly, saying what they liked about Northern money-chasers and mudsills. The fact that the Northerners scorned the duello as an immorality only convicted them of cowardice in the eyes of the Southerners, who took advantage of the situation to abuse them with intoxicating freedom. The four Northerners who had openly opposed them on the slavery issue —Hale of New Hampshire, Chase of Ohio, Hamlin of Maine, and Seward of New York—were all comparatively new men, and meek under castigation. Seward, brightest of the four, stood in the cloakroom door, smoking big cigars and smiling philosophically whenever he was the target. The Southerners regarded him as a coward.

So the session of 1851 began, as of old, with the Southerners reveling in the old game of flaying the plebeian North. On an early day, one of the Cotton patricians took up, for the luxuriant amusement of his colleagues, the subject of Ohio, a land of uncivilized backwoods louts, lowly enough to help niggers escape their masters. One gleaming sentence he concluded with the phrase "nigger-thieves."

At this point an incredible thing happened. From somewhere a voice bellowed, "You're a liar!"

The Southerner swayed on his feet as if struck by lightning. Senators everywhere turned in amazement to see who had been so lunatic. Rubbing their eyes, they saw that the offense had been committed by the innocent old judge from Ohio. He must have talked in his sleep! But no, there he sat, leveling at the fire-eater the meanest glare anyone present had ever seen, a wicked pair of small, black eyes and a hard, hard jaw.

A Northern "mud-sill" had dared to call a Southern gentleman a liar! As if coming out of a dream, the senators from the Slave States swarmed around their colleague to keep him from assassinating the insolent puppy on the spot. A few antislavery men scrambled up to protect Ben Wade, but the judge simply sat there, unwinking, waiting.

That night delegations felt him out. Would he fight if challenged?

"I am here," he answered coldly, "in a double capacity. I represent the state of Ohio and I represent Ben Wade. As a senator I am opposed to dueling, but as Ben Wade I recognize the code. I say your friend is a foul-mouthed old blackguard, but you will find that he will never notice what I have said. I will not be asked for retraction, explanation, or fight."

That night all Washington talked of the new senator from Ohio. The fire-eaters were aghast. Over the city went the appalling whisper that the innocent frontiersman hadn't brought his rifle to Washington to shoot squirrels but to shoot Southern gentlemen!

Suspicion deepened into conviction as scouts collected information about the fellow. He was rough and coarse, they learned, an ornery old skeptic, profane, blunt, contemptuous of romance and oratory, cynical, fearless, rigidly Abolitionist, no respecter of persons—and one of the best rifleshots in the Northwest. All eyes were on him as he walked to his seat the next morning, and all eyes popped as he calmly drew two pistols from his pocket, placed them in his desk, and sat down as though to say, "I'm ready."

As he had prophesied, nothing more was said of a challenge and the matter dropped, but something had happened to the spirits of men in the Senate. From that moment the antislavery cause looked up, and the road of Southern aristocrats began sloping downhill. In future, all proslavery orators were to be more or less flustered when they arose to abuse the North, and never as confident as of old, for at any moment Ben Wade might rush and rough them. His method was to affront a speaker and let it go at that. If the aggrieved party felt like fighting, there was the thought of that cold-barreled squirrel-rifle to sober him down. The Southerners might learn how to answer the other Abolitionist Senators who now followed Wade's lead, but they never learned how to handle the old judge himself.

II

For that matter, no one had ever managed him. He had come to the heights along hard ways. Born the tenth child of a Revolutionary veteran in Massachusetts in 1800, he had grown up on manual labor, poverty, and sparse schooling, a Roundhead boy destined by life, birth, and ancestry to deal the cavaliers prodigious wallops. Puritan to the last drop was his blood, his maternal grandfather having been the Reverend Michael Wigglesworth, who at Malden in 1633 composed that celebrated poem, "The Day of Doom," one of the chief documents of New England evangelism. As a boy, Ben Wade is said to have learned it by heart and to have rattled it off upon occasion, although the occasions could not have been frequent, for when, in later life, he came to the necessity of speaking in public, he was, in the beginning, the most blundering and confused of orators. Nevertheless, "The Day of Doom" could not have made the boy tender of mind, for it was a solemn and ferocious picture of a hard-hearted Jehovah dooming the unbaptized to everlasting torment:

> But get away without delay,
>   Christ pities not your cry,
> Depart to Hell; there may you dwell
>   And roar eternally.

It would be easy to overestimate "The Day of Doom" in explaining the savagery with which Ben Wade, as a man, assailed the "sin" of slavery. His training may have made him stern, but it did not make him religious, for in adulthood he was a skeptic, possibly an atheist, and his infidelism was an issue against him in his political life.

Emigrating, with the family, to Ohio in 1821, he speedily cut loose for himself, a bold, independent boy, roaming the country as a cattle-driver, working as a ditch-digger on the Erie Canal, teaching school, studying medicine (unsuccessfully) in Albany, and settling down, at twenty-five, to study law in Ohio. At thirty-one he was a partner of the mighty Joshua R. Giddings, idol of the midland Abolitionists.

Laboriously acquiring the knack of speaking to crowds and juries, Wade shared Giddings' fat law practice and followed him into politics, graduating from county attorney to state senator and to judge, arriving at the last station in 1847. Giddings' influence led him to become a bull in the china shop wherein Ohio was striving so delicately to keep peace with the neighboring Slave States. Ruthlessly he badgered the state into nullifying the laws which made it every Ohioan's duty to catch all runaway slaves and return them to their old Kentucky homes.

Single-handed in 1842, he crammed through the Legislature a bill to found a college, eventually Oberlin, where Negroes might be educated along with whites. Although the antislavery population of Ohio was in the minority, his popularity captured even some of those citizens who looked upon the Abolition cause with indifference. In the first place, he was relentlessly honest. When the firm of Giddings & Wade went bankrupt in the national panic of 1837, both men ignored the refuge of the bankruptcy laws and paid off their debts. Wade, in particular, seized the fancy of many younger men. Budding lawyers worshiped him. He fitted the frontier notion of a man, scorning good manners as effeminate, diplomats as liars, gentlemen as poseurs. Says his biographer, A. G. Riddle: "Young men combed their hair back over their heads as he did. Where he was merely frank and abrupt, they became coarse and rough; where he indulged in stronger English, they became profane. In a few years, the bar of northern Ohio was invaded by rude, swearing caricatures of the strong magnetic man."

As a judge, Wade seems to have been able. The upper courts seldom reversed him. Once when they did so, he reheard the case, decided it as before, and sent it back with the remark, "I'll give them another chance to get it right." They did.

When small cases appeared on his docket over and over without settlement, he would slap the amount at issue on the bar, saying, "Here, I'll pay the damn thing myself!"

Immensely scornful of women, as of all things of grace, Ben was suddenly bowled over, in his forty-first year, by the face of a girl rapturously upturned in a political crowd that listened to him in Ashtabula. He married her, but, so far as anyone noted, Caroline Rosekrans did not soften him toward life. He loved to sit of evenings and listen to her read, but on the street he was the same old Ben Wade, banging into offices, barging past barriers, getting what he wanted.

This was the man who came to the United States Senate in 1851 and characteristically made a thunderous début with his abrupt "You're a liar!" Never a respecter of tradition, he smashed precedents right and left. He became that rarest of senators, a leader in his first term. He thumbed his nose at all claims of seniority, gentility, and polity. With Sumner, he began poking into the tenderest parts of the slavery issue, which all the party leaders wanted hushed in order that the dividing nation might heal its sores under the salve of the recent compromises. While Sumner assailed the slaveholders with lofty righteousness, Wade began pushing them around, treating them rough, flouting them.

Nor was it only on Southerners that he loosed his caustic tongue. Douglas, who he said kowtowed to slavery, found

him most unpleasant. Once, when the Little Giant re-
marked on the floor that "the gentleman from Ohio enter-
tains a different code of morals from myself," Wade
snorted, "Morals? My God, I hope so!" At another time,
when the Senate had been listening to Douglas tearing
his heart over some evil or other for hours, Wade suddenly spoke up with, "Well, what are you going to do
about it?" Douglas turned red and sat down.

It was another jolt from Wade that so critical an observer as Judge Jeremiah Black thought "the most effective single blow ever dealt a man, a cause, or an argument
in the history of Congress." Senator George E. Badger of
North Carolina was up this day piteously bemoaning the
fact that brutal Northerners would forbid Southerners to
take their slaves with them into the free territories of
Kansas and Nebraska. What an outrage it was, he said,
that he, who longed to emigrate to the West, could not
take his dear old black mammy with him—the old mammy
who had nursed him, raised him, cared for him like a
mother! How could the North tear them apart? All but
in tears, he was producing a most sentimental effect when
Wade broke in with, "We're willing for you to take your
old mammy with you, but we're afraid that when you
get her there *you'll sell her!*" Badger went down like
Douglas.

To Senator Dixon of Kentucky, who ridiculed him for
believing a Negro the equal of a white man, Wade
snapped, "By the law of God Almighty, *your* slave is
your equal, as you'll find out at the Day of Judgment,
though probably not before—at your rate of progress."
Senator Butler of South Carolina was interrupted in his
oration on the Negroes' love for their masters with, "Yes,

they love you so well you have to have a Fugitive Slave
Law to bring 'em back!" Senator Clayton of Delaware,
wounded by characteristic thrusts, talked of challenging
the old judge, but, on hearing that Wade was polishing
his squirrel-rifle, gave up the idea.

Nettling and hectoring the fire-eaters with his inter-
ruptions, queries, belittlements, Wade expanded into
short, impromptu orations in which he warned the South
not to bully the Northern people. There was in his speech,
the tread, already, of the midland farmers who would
form Grant's and Sherman's legions, they who broke the
back of Secession. And as always, behind him in the
Middle West were rough supporters who, although not
yet quite ready for Abolition, liked to see him blow up
the Southern aristocrats. The multiplying anti-slaverites
knew him for their own as surely as they knew Charles
Sumner, even if Wade was too thrifty to put any money
into the underground railroad which helped fugitive
slaves to Canada. He was, by nature, economical to say
the least, although once, when a Negro boy came to him
begging for funds with which to buy his freedom, he
growled, "I never give to such causes; but why don't you
run away? Here's ten dollars for expenses."

III

As a hero of the frontier people, he reached his zenith
on May 23, 1856, the day after a tinder-headed South
Carolinian, Preston S. Brooks, had beaten Charles Sumner
into insensibility at his desk on the Senate floor. The affair
was a national issue overnight. War trembled in the balance, with the South crying that Brooks had taught the

insolent Yankee to keep his foul tongue off Southern people, and with the North crying that Brooks' assault was typical of the degeneracy of a civilization which talked of honor and yet used the pistol and bludgeon to settle its quarrels.

Vituperation passed back and forth as the Senate met the next day to consider the matter. Robert Toombs, of Georgia, wildest and probably ablest of the fire-eaters, certainly their captain at this session, arose and defended Brooks' attack. As he sat down, up bolted Ben Wade, "When an assassin-like, cowardly attack has been made on an unarmed man," he bellowed, "powerless to defend himself and almost murdered, and such attacks are approved by senators, it becomes a question of interest to the minority. . . . If the principle now here announced prevails, let us come armed for the contest, and although you are four to one, *I am here to meet you!*"

As he spoke, he bent toward Toombs his ugliest stare, and as he took his seat the whole Senate felt that now, at last, he would receive the challenge which he had courted so long. Certainly Toombs, the touchiest of Southerners, must fight him. After the session he was asked by Southern men if he would accept when the challenge came. Certainly! What weapons would he name? Rifles at thirty paces. "You fellows," he added, "have broken Sumner's head, and we must spunk up or you'll break all our heads. The shortest way is to kill off a few of you and I've picked on old Toombs. He'll have to challenge me. I'll take my old squirrel-rifle and, damn me, if I don't bring him down at the first crack."

Again the menace of that squirrel-rifle hung over Washington as Wade sat for two days in his home, waiting for the challenge. On the third day, he returned to his desk, felt a hand on his shoulder, and looked up into the face of Toombs. "Wade," said the fire-eater, "what's the use of two men making damned fools of themselves?"

But old Ben did not stop with this temporary victory. With Chandler of Michigan, hard-mouthed Zachariah Chandler, and Simon Cameron of Pennsylvania he swore a pact of death. Whenever a Southern senator affronted the Northern people the three were to send him challenges. "We will carry the quarrel into the coffin," they swore, and the news of their vow got around. "The tone of Southerners modified at once," said Wade, recalling it later.

Secession, growing ever heavier in the air, could not come soon enough for him. To him it was inevitable; all that he wanted was to make it plain to the seceders that there would be a terrific fight. To senators who threatened to leave the Union, he adopted the policy of extending his hand and booming, "Good-bye! Don't wait on my account!" That his attitude hastened the war cannot be doubted, for always he tormented the aristocrats. Realistic in the extreme, bald and coarse in his practicality, he would not permit the Southern romanticists to speak with the floweriness, finesse, and grace which they felt to be so basic a part of their lives. He hated such things as much as he hated jewelry.

When the break came in 1861 he was ready for it, wasting no time on reconciliation and, indeed, helping to kill the last-minute Crittenden Compromise. On the day of the first battle, Bull Run, outside Washington, he put his squirrel-rifle into a carriage and drove out to the field. Perhaps after all, he would get a chance to shoot a South-

ern gentleman. But it was his own Northerners that prevented it, thousands of Union soldiers sweeping him backward in a rout toward Washington. When the road
narrowed between impassable forests, he turned his carriage across it, marshaled his party in a thin line, set his
hat down over his ears, and flattened his jaw against the
butt of his rifle.

"Boys, we'll stop this damned runaway!" he roared;
and stop it he did, holding the flood until organized troops
relieved him. Fear-crazed fugitives backed away from
his muzzle, more terrorized by it than by the whole Confederate army, which they mistakenly believed to be at
their heels. On the way back to Washington, he blued the
air with curses. So he became the one hero of Bull Run,
the one Northerner who had done something on that awful
day. How much greater a hero he would have been in
Northern history if he had died on the field, ringed
'round with the bodies of Southern colonels!

No such luck! The days were done when he could stand
out like a Charles the Hammer, hurling back the foe.
His work of slaughtering fire-eaters was now taken over
by the army. To replace his long, lone rifle there appeared
a million muskets.

IV

Moreover, he had the misfortune, during the war, to be
measured, not against fire-eaters, but against Abraham
Lincoln. Himself a defeated aspirant for the Republican
presidential nomination in 1860, he was opposed to Lincoln on other scores. The man in the White House was
too slow, too gentle with the enemy, put too many Northern Democrats in office, was too backward about freeing

the slaves, too weak to confiscate rebel property. Was he proslave at heart? Wade wondered.

When Lincoln ignored Congress in making his plans for reconstructing the South, Wade called him a tyrant and sneered at senators who "waited for the royal pleasure" before voting. "Our system of government is a failure," he growled. "Congress and the judiciary are only instruments in the hands of the Executive."

Finally, when Lincoln rejected the Radicals' vengeful plan of Reconstruction, Wade broke loose in one of the most amazing performances in the history of party politics. Uniting with Henry Winter Davis of Maryland, Lincoln's fiercest Republican foe in the lower house, the old Senator issued the famous Wade-Davis Manifesto, which, appearing at the height of the presidential campaign, assailed the head of the ticket as a usurper who, swollen with personal ambition, "strides headlong into anarchy." So thunderous was the blast that it overshot its mark, rallied the voters to Lincoln, and knocked Davis out of his seat in Congress. Wade, standing for re-election in Ohio, lost his constituents and was re-elected by Democratic legislators who evidently thought him a better trouble-maker for the administration than any Democrat they might select.

Lincoln, who knew all that Wade knew of retort, but who made his replies with humor, deflated the old judge upon occasion as the judge had deflated the Southerners. Once, when the Radicals' uproar was at its tensest, Wade left his office in the Capitol and stamped the long mile to the White House to abuse Lincoln. Butting his way into the President's study, he announced, "This government is drifting to hell!"

"Yes, Senator," answered Lincoln dryly, "it's only about a mile from there this minute."

As he spoke, he pointed a long forefinger at the window, through which could be seen the Capitol dome against the sky. Wade went back to his office. Whether the story be fact or legend it matters not, for it points a sad truth: the bellower who had deafened the fire-eaters was worsted by a man with a drawl.

Baffled and sore, Wade, dominating powerful committees, harassed Lincoln throughout the war. At the end, when Lincoln adroitly put all the surrendering Southern gentlemen out of Radical reach, he was beside himself. The worst of it was that Lincoln had four more years to serve, years in which, Wade feared, the reviving South would reunite with Northern Copperheads to rule again.

Then came the stroke which must have made even skeptical old Ben Wade believe in the Jehovah of the Reverend Michael Wigglesworth. Lincoln was murdered and Andrew Johnson, bitter enemy of Southern aristocrats, took the helm. Old Ben, seizing the new President's hand, exulted: "By the gods, we'll have no trouble running the government now!" Later he was advising Johnson, "I would hang or exile ten or twelve of those fellows [the Confederate leaders]. I think I could make it thirteen, just a baker's dozen."

Although named an honorary pallbearer at Lincoln's funeral, he did not attend, his friends explaining that he hated the excesses of funeral woe. More likely, the reason lay in his traditional desire "to carry the quarrel into the coffin."

But his joy over Lincoln's death was short. His enemy refused somehow to stay in the tomb. The dead President's gentle scheme for reconstructing the South stole back to capture Johnson, and as Johnson vetoed, one after another, the harsh measures which Congress prepared for "the conquered territories," Wade turned frenzied fanatic. Even those senators who had forgiven his harshness for the sake of the iron strength he had supplied to Union spirit during the war now thought him only malignant and brutal. Shame left him. Once, when the Radicals were massing to override Johnson's veto of their oppressive Civil Rights Bill, delay was asked to permit a sick Johnson-man to arrive in time to vote. Wade objected. "If God Almighty has stricken one member so that he cannot be here to uphold the dictation of a despot," he roared, "I thank Him for His interposition, and I will take advantage of it if I can."

What he, with the other Radicals, was plotting now was the removal of Johnson. And it was Ben Wade himself who was waiting to take the Presidency. As president *pro tem* of the Senate and acting Vice-President of the United States, he was next in succession. Let him sit in the White House and the Southern gentlemen might indeed despair!

The impeachment trial came on, and the old judge, now sixty-seven years old, white of hair and eyebrows, sat waiting with a harder light than ever in his cold, black, unwinking eyes. Brazenly he counted himself already in the White House and openly arranged his Cabinet. Unless he won this goal, he was through, for Ohio had soured of his venom and elected another man to fill his shoes the coming December. If he could grasp the Presidency, there would be time, in the remaining year of the term, to juggle patronage so that he might assure himself of the vice-presidential nomination, at least, in the 1868 campaign. But by now he was his own worst enemy. His reptilian hate boomeranged as it had in the days of the Wade-Davis Manifesto. As he had then strengthened Lincoln, so now he strengthened Johnson. Many a Republican senator, wavering on which way to vote on impeachment, shuddered to think of vicious old Ben in the White House. His character helped Johnson. Impeachment failed by one vote.

So Ben Wade missed the Presidency. He sat a little longer in the Senate, which he had bullied for seventeen years. His enemies—Lincoln, Johnson, and the Southern gentlemen—were all down, dead, or ruined, but what was he? Only another lame-duck of Washington. He was out of it when, at last, Radical Reconstruction descended full force upon the Southern people. In the Presidential campaign of 1868, he agreed to stump Ohio for Grant, whom he distrusted. Hadn't Grant said, "Let us have peace"? Privately, Wade dismissed him with a sneer. "Whenever I'd talk politics, he'd talk horses." Still, Republican success would mean a Radical Congress.

In 1870 prissy Schuyler Colfax, the Vice-President, recommended Wade as a lobbyist to Jay Cooke, and it is probable that Ben did some work for this financier. He became attorney for the Northern Pacific Railroad. Hot human issues, however bitter, ceased to dominate him.

Finally, he lent himself to Grant's expansionist dream of annexing Santo Domingo, and headed an investigating committee that visited the island and reported favorably upon the plan. On board ship he was the same testy autocrat as of old, storming at "the crazy buggists" who, as the scientific section of the commission, delayed the homeward voyage while they collected tropical plants.

He simmered slowly down, living until 1878. But just before the end his old spirit flared. Rutherford B. Hayes, stepping into the Presidency, began to loose the chains of Reconstruction. The Radicals had spent their venom. A new day had come. But Ben Wade was still blind. Savagely he lashed out at Hayes for his mercy, denouncing him as he had denounced Lincoln and Johnson, but his words only re-echoed back at him in his own death-chamber.

The Secret Evangel
of Otto McFeely

ALTHOUGH the village of Oak Park, Illinois, has never recognized the fact, and may not even now when confronted with the evidence, it contains a remarkable missionary—one who has toiled without expectation of gain, here or hereafter—a most unusual missionary sitting on the front porch at 200 Forest Avenue.

He is Otto McFeely, who, having retired from the editorship of the local weekly, *Oak Leaves,* takes his slippered ease these days and thinks back on the time when he coursed midwestern roads, spreading his particular benefaction.

I stumbled upon his true mission one summer afternoon twenty years ago. Up to then I had shared the general belief that he was merely a busy editor who took motor drives for recreation. I knew, of course, that he had brought into being the Mosquito Abatement District, but there was self in that crusade, for he had been angered at the welts the insects had raised upon his infant daughter. And his success in fathering the Mothers' Pension Law had been prompted in part by his desire to promote something impressive for his bosom friend, Judge Neal, to head up and orate about. What I didn't know about was McFeely's secret evangel.

You would never suspect it to watch him in his office.

There, all week, he was polite to the Puritans who brought him their wholesome items of news for publication, clergymen, deacons, presidents of ladies' clubs, Kiwanians, all bringing announcements and reports of their manifold charities and public betterments. But of a Saturday or Sunday he'd go off in his Ford alone. Sometimes he'd take me along, and the first time he did I learned why he went.

He stopped the car on this hot July Saturday, and stepping out, shouted loudly at a farmer plowing corn. The man stopped his team and turned his ear to listen. McFeely cleared his throat and, enunciating with careful clarity, informed the stranger that he was many kinds of a beast, fiend, robber, decadent, and that his ancestry was shameful and his future life one of eternal damnation.

The farmer stepped off his plow, cupped a work-hardened hand behind a sunburnt ear and called, "What did you say?"

Patiently McFeely went through it all again, adding some new and more loathsome epithets for good measure.

Even at this distance I could see the farmer's face flush, as he stiffened, clenched his fists, and tried to form choking retorts. Before he could make any suitable rejoinder, however, his insulter had popped back into the Ford and was driving away.

After a short silence, I asked McFeely, "Was that called for?"

He sighed and wearily said, "You are too obtuse for me to fool with. However, I'll explain what I'd think anybody could see:

"That man is vegetating, making those endless rounds of the monotonous corn rows, behind two horses day after day. Life is dull to him, and dull for his wife in that house over there because he has nothing to say when he comes in for dinner and supper. He's in a rut and so is she. But I can bring him, and her, temporary relief if not a cure.

"At noon today he'll hurry in from the barn to tell her about the gross insult he received. She'll be mad, too. It does people's souls good to get mad. They'll stay mad for weeks, hashing over the cruelty done him, wondering who it could have been and if the scoundrel will be back. They'll be live, thinking, feeling persons for a time. Life will become vivid for them.

"You see, this thing would be no good unless it were a purely gratuitous insult. It must be simon-pure outrage. Its merit lies in the completeness of its injustice."

A handsome fellow with a Ronald Colman mustache and a dashing air, McFeely used, and probably still uses, his romantic aura to help him in his mission. For example, I have ridden slowly with him through sleepy Illinois towns on a Sunday afternoon and seen him suddenly tip his hat gallantly to a woman of fifty who sat on her front porch dully looking out at nothing. McFeely's dark eyes would gleam with grave tenderness upon her as we rolled past.

Then, just before we went from view, he'd look back with restrained yearning as she, leaning forward on her frozen rocking chair, would be peering after him.

Did he know her? Had he ever seen her before? Certainly not, and would, moreover, never come this way again, either.

"But," said he, "she'll wonder for weeks who that was. Could it have been that visiting tenor—after choir practice—thirty years ago—?

"She'll be tender to her husband for probably sixty days all on account of this, and full of tolerance for sinners whenever her shrewish neighbor women start gossiping."

Upon rare occasions McFeely has been able to cast the sweet cloak of his evangel over quarreling husbands and wives.

"Driving along, I keep looking for them," he told me once, "Sunday drivers, dressed up and suddenly sore because he asked her if she had turned out the fire under the water heater before they left. What I do then is pull alongside, scrape fenders, holler for a halt, and then lean out and call, 'Turn around and go home. It's hell for you Sunday drivers on these arterial highways. You'll smash that beautiful car and,' here I look past him at his wife, 'you'll kill that lovely wife of yours.'

"Then I step on the gas quick and get away, leaving them to forget their differences in the mingled emotions my solicitude and insolence have forced upon them."

That Cold, Hard Eye

ONE of the best drama criticisms ever written by that best of all American drama critics, Percy Hammond, was about *Champagne, Sec,* Dwight Deere Wiman's revival of *Die Fledermaus* in 1934.

How Hammond wrote his piece so well I never knew, nor will now ever learn, for Percy is dead. I always meant to ask him, but whenever I saw him we talked so much about Morgan's Raid that I never got around to it.

I never wondered at his ability to write well, but I could never see how he got his mind back on the show after what he said between the end of the play and his arrival at his office in the New York *Herald Tribune,* where he wrote his reviews in longhand.

As we came out of the theater that night, he began talking about John Sherman, one-time senator from Ohio, secretary of the treasury, and brother of General William Tecumseh.

"When I was a boy," said Percy, "a boy about sixteen in Cadiz, Ohio, I was in trouble. As things turned out later, I wasn't in trouble. I only imagined I was. Anyway, I was scared. I lit out for Washington, D. C., to see if I could get a job in the Government Printing Office. I could set type.

"There were lines of men standing for those jobs, all union men, which I was not. No jobs in town, even if I could have got a union card, which I couldn't. I knew nobody in the city. The day came when I had nothing to eat all day long, and in the evening I was standing on Pennsylvania Avenue, whipped out.

"My eye saw a team of fine horses drawing a carriage and in the carriage was a face that was familiar—a hard, cold face. It was John Sherman's, the senator from Ohio.

"I said to myself that there went the meanest man in America, the man my father back home had fought in his newspaper and denounced up and down.

"But it was the first face that I had seen from Ohio, and I was famished. So I found out where the senator lived and walked to it that evening. I rang the bell at about nine-forty-five. The butler said the senator never saw anyone without appointment. I argued. He started to shut the door.

"I pushed in and said, in what was evidently a wild voice, 'I've got to see him. My father and my grandfather marched to the sea behind his brother!'

"Then I fainted.

"When I came to, I was sitting on a black horsehair sofa with the butler giving me a glass of water. Someone was beside me on the sofa. I looked around. It was John Sherman and his cold, blue eye was on me. I drew away.

" 'I'm sorry,' I said. 'I'll go.'

"The senator fixed his mean face right on me and said, 'I was coming downstairs when I heard you call out. Who are you?'

"I told him who my father was and I could see him nod as he recalled his political enemy. 'Well,' said he, 'come in and tell me more about Ohio. You know,' he said, fixing his icy glare on his butler, 'I always have a glass of milk about this time of night. Come in and talk to me while I drink it.'

"We went out slowly into the dining room and there appeared two bowls of milk and two piles of bread. He sat down and commenced to eat and so did I.

"He'd shake his head whenever I'd explain how I wanted a job. Finally he got up and I got my hat and said good-bye. I could tell by his face he was thinking about the names my father had called him. At the door he suddenly held out a five-dollar bill and put his gimlet eye on me.

" 'Take this,' he said, and when I shook my head, he growled, 'It's a LOAN.' I took it and he went on, 'And if you're around this way tomorrow drop in. There are no jobs in Washington, but drop around.'

"I knew he was pleased in his hard, hard heart to see a Hammond squirm, but I went back the next day. He was in, face sourer than ever, and he talked to me about what a terrible place Washington was and how much better everything was in Cadiz. I thanked him, said I'd pay him back as quickly as I could and got up to go. He said, 'Oh, by the way, I happened to be at the Government Printing Office this afternoon and overheard them say they had lots of vacancies.'

"His hypocritical old eye never wavered as he told that bald-faced lie.

" 'Go there tomorrow. There's a job for you waiting. Say I sent you.' He turned brusquely away, and I turned toward the door. Then he said, 'Wait.'

"I turned back. I knew it was coming. He'd been leading me on and was going to spring the blow right now.

" 'Oh, here it is,' he said, and handed me a card. 'I had

business over at the typographical union today and happened to think of you and I got 'em to give you a card. Your hours will be daytime. You'd make more money working nights, but the night crew is a hard one. You work days. Good-bye.'

"I couldn't thank him, and opened the door.

" 'Wait!' he said again, and I waited. He was coming toward me with naked hate in his expression. 'How old did you say you were?'

" 'Sixteen,' I answered, my heart going down, for here the catch was coming at last.

" 'Sixteen,' he said. 'All right. The day you're twenty-one you get out of this damn town and never come back. Good-bye.'

"I never saw him again. But the day I was twenty-one, I left Washington for good."

My Biggest Baseball Day*

WHEN the bleacher gates at Shibe Park in Philadelphia were thrown open on the morning of October 24, 1911, I was in the mob that went whooping toward the front seats. I got one in right field because the Philadelphians raced for left field to sit as close as possible to the bench of their worshiped Athletics, for the World Series at that moment stood two games to one for the American League's Connie Mack against the National League's John McGraw, and Philadelphia was loud and passionate in the confidence that now they would get revenge for the bitter dose—four games to one, three shutouts—these same New York Giants had given them six years before.

Me, I wanted to get as close to the Giants as possible, and found a place at the rail close to the empty chairs which would that afternoon become the Giants' bull pen. My whole adolescence had been devoted, so far as baseball went—and it went a long way to an Indiana farmboy —to the Giants and to their kingly pitcher, "Big Six," the great, the incomparable Christy Mathewson. I hadn't had the courage to cut classes in the near-by college and go to the first game of the series at Shibe Park. But today I had. Things were desperate. Up in New York's Polo Grounds to start this, the World Series, Mathewson had

won—2 to 1—giving but five hits and demonstrating that
with twelve years of Herculean toil behind him he was
practically as invincible as when in 1905 he had shut out
these same Athletics three times.

It had looked like 1905 over again; then, in the second
game, the A's long, lean yokel third baseman, J. Franklin
Baker, had suddenly and incredibly knocked a home run
off Rube Marquard, the Giants' amazing young pitcher.
Baker, who had hit only nine homers all season, had
tagged the twenty-two-year-old Giant and two runs had
come in—and the final had stood 3 to 1.

The papers which I read in the bleachers, as the morning wore on, were still full of that home run and its after-
math.

From the start of the series the newspapers had been
publishing syndicated articles signed by Giant and Athletic
stars—the real start of the "ghost writers" whose spurious
trade flourished so long but which the better papers in
time eliminated. And in the article signed by Mathewson
the day after Marquard's disaster it had been said that
Rube had lost the game by failing to obey orders. The
article rebuked the boy for throwing Baker the high outside pitch he liked, instead of the low fast one he didn't
like and which McGraw had ordered.

The rebuke had been a sensation which grew in the
third game when Baker had hit another homer off
Mathewson himself, and had been the main wrecker of
the great man's long sway over the A's. Up to the ninth
inning of that third game Matty had kept command.
Always when the Athletics had got men on bases he had
turned on his magic. As he went to the bench at the end
of the eighth, New York had risen and given him a tre-

mendous ovation, for in forty-four innings of World Series play, 1905 and 1911, he had allowed the Mackmen exactly one run—and the A's were hitters, indeed. Their season's average for 1911 had been .297.

Then in the ninth, Eddie Collins had gone out, and only two men had stood between Matty and his fifth series victory over his victims. Up had come Baker with the American League fans begging him to do to Matty what he had done to Marquard—and, incredible as it seemed, he had done this.

As home runs go, it hadn't been much more than a long fly that sailed into the convenient right-field stand at the Polo Grounds, but it had gone far enough to tie the score and give Baker a nickname for life—"Home Run" Baker.

Snodgrass, the Giants' center fielder, one of the smartest and greatest of base runners, had ripped Baker's trousers almost off him, sliding into third in the first of the tenth inning. With McGraw snarling, railing, jeering from the coaching line, the Giants made no secret of their hatred of Baker. To them he was merely a lucky lout, a greenhorn who had by sheer accident homered off the two top pitchers of the season.

But Baker had hit again, a scratch single, in the eleventh which had been part of the making of the run which had won, and Marquard, in his "ghosted" article, had quipped at Mathewson's advice.

All that was in everybody's mind—and mine—as on October 24 the fourth game came up. The papers had had time to chew the sensation over and over, for it had rained for a week after the third game and now, with

seven days' rest, Mathewson was to try again—this time
in Shibe Park.

The long delay hadn't cooled excitement. The press
box was still as crowded as at the opening game. This was
the first World Series to be handled in the modern publicity fashion—the first to have as many as fifty teleg-
raphers on the job—the first to wire the game play by
play to points as distant as Havana, Cuba—the first to
which newspapers in the Far West and South sent their
own writers. And though the A's now had a lead of two
games to one, the threat of the Giants was still great
enough to keep fever high.

It was a little after one o'clock when my long vigil
ended. Onto the field came the Giants with their immemorial swagger, chips still on their shoulders—the
cocky, ornery, defiant men of Muggsy McGraw—the
rip-roaring demons who had, that season of 1911, set a
record of 347 stolen bases—a record which would stand
for another thirty-five years without any other club's
ever coming nearer to it than the Senators' 288 in 1913.

And here at long last they were! I knew them from
their pictures as, clad in dangerous black, they came
strutting across toward their dugout. McGraw had dressed
his men in sable uniforms back in 1905 when he had
humbled the Athletics, and he was playing hunches now.

Muggsy was first—stocky, hard-eyed. Behind him
came slim, handsome Snodgrass, striding as became a
genius at getting hit by pitched balls and in scaring in-
fielders with his flashing spikes. Then came swart, ominous
Larry Doyle; lantern-jawed Art Fletcher; Buck Herzog,
whose nose curved like a scimitar; lithe little Josh Devore;
burly Otis Crandall; flat-faced, mahogany-colored Chief

Meyers, the full-blooded Indian; Fred Merkle, all muscles, even in his jaws, a lionheart living down the most awful bonehead blunder ever made in baseball.

Then came Marquard, six feet three, his sharp face and slitlike eyes smiling—his head tilting to the left at the top of a long wry neck—Marquard the meteoric! At nineteen years of age he had been bought at a record price from Indianapolis and had immediately flopped two straight years for McGraw, becoming the nationally goatish "$11,000 lemon." Then, this 1911, he had flamed out, won twenty-four games, and become the "$11,000 beauty."

As the Giants began to toss the ball around, I couldn't see my hero, the Mathewson whom I had come to see, the great one who, from the time I was nine, I had pretended I was, playing ball in the Indiana cow pasture, throwing his famous "fade-away" which, for me, never came off. Then, suddenly, there he was, warming up and growling, "Who am I working for, the Giants or the photographers," as the cameramen not twenty feet from my popeyed head, begged him for poses.

I was let down for a minute. He didn't speak like a demigod, but as I stared, he looked it, all the same. He held his head high, and his eye with slow, lordly contempt swept the Athletics as they warmed up across the field. He was thirty-one, all bone and muscle and princely poise.

Surely he would get those Athletics today and put the Giants back in the running. Surely his unique "fade-away," the curve that broke backward, his speed, his snapping curve, his fabulous brain couldn't be stopped.

It had been luck that had beaten him in the last game. Now he'd get them.

My eye never left him till the bell rang and he strode, hard but easy, with the swing of the aristocrat, into the dugout, and little Josh Devore went up to hit.

Josh singled, Doyle tripled, Snodgrass scored Larry with a long fly. Black figures were flying everywhere. The big copper-colored Chief Bender on Mack's mound was wobbling, and when the side was finally out he practically ran for the dugout. Later, we learned, he had run in to cut off bandages from his ribs, tape from a recent injury. After that he was to be unbeatable.

Up came the Athletics, Matty, as though in princely disdain, fanned the first two men. The third man, Eddie Collins, singled. Here came Baker, his sun-tanned face tense, his bat flailing—the air thick with one word from 25,000 throats, "Homer! Homer!"

Matty studied him as a scientist contemplates a beetle, then struck him out! What I yelled, I don't know. All I remember is standing there bellowing and paying no heed to the wadded newspapers the Athletic fans around me threw. It was wonderful!

In the fourth, Baker came up to start it and doubled. Dannie Murphy doubled, Harry Davis doubled. Ira Thomas hit a sacrifice fly—three runs. It couldn't be. Up came Baker again in the fifth with Collins on first, and another double boomed across the diamond. I saw Snodgrass eventually stop the ball, but he didn't really have it in his glove at all. It had stuck in my gullet.

Right in front of me an unthinkable thing happened. Hooks Wiltse, the southpaw, began warming up for the Giants. Was Matty knocked out? Another figure rose from the bull pen. Rube Marquard. He didn't warm up, he only strolled up and down, a great sardonic grin on his face. The fans around me were screaming at him, "You're even with Matty now, Rube! He won't tell you what to pitch any more!" etc., etc. Rube smirked at them.

Matty got by without more scores, but in the seventh, with a man on third, Christy walked Baker on four intentional balls, and Shibe Park's walls waved in a cyclone of "boos." I wished I was dead.

The eighth. A pinch hitter went up for Mathewson. I was sorry I hadn't died in the seventh.

Finally it was all over.

I walked out through 24,000 of the most loathsome individuals ever created—all jeering at Mathewson, all howling Baker's virtues. I dragged my feet this way and that trying to escape the currents of fans. At the end of a dolorous mile I stopped at a saloon. I had never had a drink. Now was the time.

"Beer," I said, in the voice of Poe's raven.

"You ain't twenty-one," the bartender rasped. Then he took a second look, saw that I was a hundred, and splashed a great stein in front of me.

I took one swallow. It was bitter, just as bitter as everything else in the world. I laid down a nickel and walked out. Every step of the way downtown I kept telling myself that in my coffin, some day, there'd be only room for one thing besides myself—my hatred of the Athletics.

But what I started out to tell was about my greatest day in baseball. That came three years later, October 9, 1914, when the lowly, despised Boston Braves wallowed, humbled, trampled, laughed at the lofty Athletics to the tune of 7 to 1. Hoarse and happy, I came out of Shibe

Park, spent hours hunting that same saloon, but I couldn't find it. It had to be that one. What I wanted to do was to walk in all alone—find nobody else in there—order two beers, and when the bartender looked inquiringly at the extra one, say to him in a condescending voice, "Oh, that? That's for Mathewson."

The Battle of Kilpatrick's Pants

"If you want to smell hell, just jine the cavalry,
If you want to have fun, just jine the cavalry."

THE words of this Confederate cavalry song must have risen to plague that squad of Southern horsemen who, on the ninth of March, 1865, lay beside a North Carolina road watching a cavalcade of Union troopers ride by. The song had been a proud one in the first years of the Civil War, but of late it had died on Secession tongues. Hell smelled a little too strong, nowadays, and it was plain that the Northern horsemen were having all the fun. For instance, here were the blue-coated troopers parading gaily home from a foraging trip with their saddlebags bulging with hams or dripping honey.

Things had come to this pass all over the South. Up in Virginia, the Confederate cavalry was demoralized, its idolized leader "Jeb" Stuart dead at Yellow Tavern. In Mississippi, General Forrest, greatest of Southern horse-captains, had been at last defeated and his riders scattered. And here, in North Carolina, General Joe Wheeler's cavalrymen were dodging about the country pursued by the "vandal" riders of Judson H. Kilpatrick, that savage, little rooster of a man who commanded Sherman's horse. The mark of "Kil" lay on Georgia and South Carolina— smoking ruins, desolate fields, gutted granaries.

And it was this most personal of their foes, Kilpatrick himself, who now passed the Confederate scouts who sulked in the bushes. The hateful fellow was lolling back in a captured carriage, his head jolting softly in the lap of a beautiful girl, his sideburns waving on either side of his impish face. Hams, victory, honey—and girls! Everything that a cavalryman wanted, everything that a horseman by virtue of his romantic calling had a right to expect of an idolatrous world.

There could have been nothing but gall in the craws of the Confederate scouts as they spurred away to take the bad news to their commanding officer, Wade Hampton, who had lately been sent to supervise Wheeler and instill some fire-eating tactics into the drooping horsemen. Both General Hampton and his lieutenant, Wheeler, were spoiling to get their hands on Kilpatrick "the ravager." For months they had been trading bitter words and bullets with the cocky Yank, and his tart jeers and confident rides were growing hard to endure. Consequently, they rejoiced to hear that their rival was off guard, frolicking with women.

The next night they struck the village where Kilpatrick had camped, and, after the fashion of professional cavalrymen, failed to look where they were going, colliding ludicrously with a battery of artillery parked in the street. This cost them their fine Southern momentum and gave the Yankees time to hop out of bed and leg it to the swamps where Kilpatrick's horses were picketed. Even after such delay, the attackers almost caught little "Kil." Battering in the door of the house where he slept, they found themselves embraced at the knees by a lovely female in scant nightwear and flowing hair. While she begged for her life, they brushed past her on into the bedroom only to find the window open and no sign of Kilpatrick but his pants.

At that moment the Union commander was bounding toward the swamps in his shirt-tail, cursing no doubt most horribly since that was his custom on occasions far less irritating.

For a time the Southerners enjoyed themselves in plunder and had just harnessed horses to the captured cannon when a storm of bareback riders burst upon them. "Kil" had rallied his veterans and now led them to the countercharge in his underdrawers. There was a brief rough-and-tumble fight, then the Confederates disappeared, abandoning the cannon, the little town grew quiet again, and life, sleep—and love—went on as before.

This celebrated conflict, which was too minor to ever have a name other than the colloquial "Battle of Kilpatrick's Pants," may be taken as a fair sample of how the cavalry had fun and smelled hell in the Civil War— a maximum of noise, a minimum of casualties, much haste, whooping, dash, and blunder, then a sudden end to it all, with loud echoes of victory emanating from both sides for weeks thereafter—but little of military import consummated.

The sad truth seems to be that despite the incessant hurrahs that went up for the armed centaurs, North and South, during and after the Civil War, the cavalry as a vital military arm had, in those very years, begun to die. Cool realists among the military experts of the day, notably the penetrating William Tecumseh Sherman, seemed to sense, if not to foresee, the virtual disappearance which would come to the cavalry within a half century.

No such vision of the future disturbed the newspaper

correspondents and popular historians of the 'Sixties. They tore open their shirts the better to cry the glories of horsemen. The melodrama inherent in the very idea of desperate riders, flashing hell-to-split through the enemy's land, burning and slashing in sudden coups and daring surprises, was an easy thing for a reporter to write about and still easier for the people at home to understand. Infantry and artillery campaigns, by which military matters were really determined, were so vast, so tedious, so complex, that correspondents found as much difficulty in explaining them as readers did in comprehending them. The man-on-horseback was another matter—a traditional hero, ready-made and at hand. A slogging foot-soldier was only a dull worthy by comparison, far beneath the equestrian in both social and romantic scales.

In the South particularly was the cavalier an aristocrat. Such an idea had been woven into the sectional mind by tradition and heredity. Having read Sir Walter Scott's novels to excess, the Southerners thought of a horseman as a chivalric knight, fit rightfully to lord it over the plodding yeoman who did the dirty work. It was Ivanhoe whom many a Southern mind visioned when it read of the cavalry exploits of Stuart, Hampton, Wheeler, Forrest, or the Lees (Fitzhugh and W. H. F.), during the Civil War. And there was scarcely less romanticism with which the North rhapsodized upon occasion over Sheridan, Pleasanton, Merritt, Custer, Grierson, or Kilpatrick.

A most significant detail in this naïve glorification of the cavalryman was the entrance of a Virginian, James Ewell Brown Stuart, into West Point with the class of 1854. "Beauty" Stuart he was nicknamed owing to his peculiar lack of chin, and although he acquired popularity by his kindness and manly conduct, the nickname must have hurt, for soon after graduation he grew a magnificent set of whiskers which remedied his appearance completely. With this acquisition he appeared as a remarkable, handsome fellow, gallant and winning, a great favorite with the ladies and the proud owner of a more satisfactory nickname, "Jeb."

Taking command of Robert E. Lee's cavalry early in the Civil War, he speedily gave the lie to the old superstition that chinless men have no force of character. If anything, Stuart displayed too much decision, being often absent on dare-devil and self-inspired raids when Lee needed him for the slower, grubbier tasks by which campaigns were to be won.

It was Stuart's spectacular equestrian feats in the summer of '62 that made Southern and Northern population "cavalry-minded." In June Jeb led his riders entirely around the huge Yankee army which threatened Richmond, and, on arriving home, he found himself the man of the hour. To the Confederacy he was the *beau idéal* of a cavalier, perfect example of the Southern genius for war. Horsemen by tradition, occupation, and ideals, the Southern aristocrats saw in Jeb's triumph the proof that the road to victory lay in enlisting more and ever more cavalry. They felt that when there were enough Confederate horsemen, the peasant footmen of the North must fall weakly underfoot. The North was also fired by Stuart's brilliance to demand that Union cavalry be increased to stop such affronts and, furthermore, to practice similar raids upon the enemy. The Yankees wanted aristocratic warriors, too.

Military experts in both Washington and Richmond

knew that Stuart's action had accomplished nothing to justify such extravagant praise. Some stores had been burned, some information gleaned, some recruits terrified, but no irreparable damage done. The responsible militarists of both sides were West Pointers who had started out in the war on the scientific theory that while cavalry might destroy the enemy's depots, wagons and trains, guard communications, and watch his movements, it could not be relied upon to decide major issues.

Nevertheless, the popular imagination was so inspired that when Stuart, in August '62, swooped round the Union army again, this time entering the tents and capturing the spare clothing of its general, John Pope, the authorities on both sides of the Potomac had to enlarge their horse squadrons.

For the next two years the Yankee horsemen tried to imitate their rivals, only to find themselves outridden and outfought most consistently. The causes were not hard to locate. Southerners, coming to the service from agrarian life, were far better acquainted with the saddle than were the bulk of Union cavalrymen who—especially those of the East—hailed from the cities. Northern mechanics, shoe clerks, hatters, felt a keen desire to mount horses and ride through the war like gentlemen, while Northern farmboys, as a class, shunned the cavalry. Especially was this true in the West where, as sons of self-sufficient pioneers, they had never suspected that a man could acquire social prominence by climbing onto a horse. Also, from arduous experience with work-animals they knew the drudgery that attended the care of a horse. Westerners preferred to walk through the war with only themselves to "do" for. So they sat on cantonment fences laughing at the town boys drill. Current gossip had it that when one horse-recruit fell off his horse he took four comrades with him. Unable to manage their mounts and ignorant of how to feed, water, or curry them properly, the Northern centaurs, up to the middle of 1863, were treated by their enemies with contempt. As a class they were brave enough, but defeat was far commoner than victory.

Quartermaster General Meigs, who had to supply horses for the Union army, grew angry at the nonchalance with which riders killed off their mounts in senseless rides and careless pasturing. Briskly he told General Rosecrans, "No government can keep 120 regiments of cavalry mounted while such a system is tolerated. They have killed off ten times as many horses for us as for the rebels." He ordered that, henceforth, all cavalrymen be taught the A B C's of their art . . . to never move their horses off a walk unless they saw an enemy before or behind, to travel only so far as to not fatigue their horses, to rest in a pasture during the heat of the day, to never pass a bridge without burning it, a telegraph wire without cutting it, a horse without stealing or shooting it, nor a Negro without reading to him the President's Emancipation Proclamation.

To further reform the Union cavalry of the East, General Joseph E. Hooker, "Fighting Joe," who was enthroned in January, 1863, started from the premise implied in the epigram attributed to him, "Whoever saw a dead cavalryman?", and progressed until he had the force in fair order. It was not, however, until the spring of 1864 that the Yankee riders could hold their own with the Confederate horsemen. In April of that year, Grant appointed an infantry officer, Philip Sheridan, to reform the cavalry attached to the Army of the Potomac, and the realistic little newcomer taught his men to behave more like foot soldiers and to dismount for serious engagements and fight behind breastworks. Such common-sense methods, coupled with the general decline in Southern morale, made the Union cavalry supreme in the last months of the war.

No American cavalry, though, was ever so near the popular ideal as were Jeb Stuart's Confederates in midsummer, 1863. Well-mounted, bristling with success, they were the despair of the North. And yet, it was this very command that demonstrated most clearly the essential defect of cavalry—theatricals.

To Stuart was assigned the all-important task of "scouting the enemy" when Lee, flushed with two years of victory, decided to invade Pennsylvania. Crossing the Potomac in July, "Marse Robert" sent Jeb on ahead to become the eyes of the army.

But human nature seems to have decreed, long ago, that a man cannot get on a horse without making a fool of himself. The elevation seems to be too much for his intellectual equilibrium.

Stuart, suffering from what Lee's intimate, General Long, described as either mistaken orders or too much "love of the *éclat* of a bold raid," dashed off on an independent operation of his own, lost touch with his commander, and did not return for eight days. In that time, poor Lee, stumbling about the enemy's land "with his eyes out," had been drawn into defeat at Gettysburg, and soon had no use for Stuart except to cover the army's retreat into Virginia. This Jeb did, bravely enough, sticking to his assignment for several weeks; then his unteachable spirit broke over the traces.

Lee, observing how his pursuer, General Meade, could be trapped during the maneuvers, ordered up Stuart's cavalry for the attack. But the cavalry was gone again! Stuart had dashed off to raid a Union wagon train and had tangled himself ignominiously between two blue infantry columns. By hiding his men in the woods for a day and night, he did manage to bring them off intact—a feat which his riders and the public hailed as another instance of his brilliance. But there was no rejoicing at Lee's headquarters where the sober militarists knew what Jeb's absence had meant.

A little earlier, Joe Hooker, fighting Lee at Chancellorsville, had been similarly handicapped by the absence of his horse-chief, Stoneman, at the very moment that the Union cavalry was needed most desperately to gather information. Stoneman was away on a raid, seeking fame.

This trait of horsemen was shrewdly perceived by the judicious Northern general, Jacob D. Cox, who wrote after the war, "The use of cavalry in raids, which were the fashion, was an amusement that was very costly to both sides. Since Stuart's ride around McClellan's army in 1862, every cavalry commander yearned to distinguish himself by some such excursion, and chafed at the comparatively obscure but useful work of learning the detailed positions and movements of an opposing army by outpost and patrol work. . . . As to raids, on both sides the game was never worth the candle. Men and horses were used up wholesale without doing any permanent damage to the enemy."

The most effective raid of the war, viewed from the

standpoint of military results, was Sheridan's through the Shenandoah Valley in 1864, although, properly speaking, it was not a raid so much as a great campaign in which infantry, artillery, and cavalry joined.

Through the Official Records of the war runs the evidence that the general psychology of the cavalryman was opposed to military effectiveness. What he wanted to be was a "beau sabreur"—and what his superiors needed was a mounted rifleman. There was a sigh of regret when his gleaming sword was taken from him in the last years of the war and the repeating carbine substituted. He could not, however, object for, in private, the troopers confessed that their sabers had lopped off more of their own horses' ears than enemy heads.

Also, the cavalryman wanted to race his horse around the country and break women's hearts. What the military experts needed was a combination reporter and section hand. Practical strategy found best use for the horseman, not in fighting but in shrewd observations of enemy movements and in destroying railroads. He could best serve his country by burning railroad ties, heating the iron rails red-hot, then twisting them around trees until nothing but a rolling-mill could restore their usefulness. But such duties involved manual labor, a work better fitted for those yokels, the infantry. An aristocrat naturally shunned such grinding toil whenever his General was looking the other way.

Sherman, whose experience with cavalry is the most impressive index of its worth, said repeatedly, "The cavalry has not the industry to damage a railroad seriously. Usually it can be repaired faster than they can damage it."

Shrewd observer that he was, Sherman depended upon this defect in the cavalryman's character to protect the Union army during his drive on Atlanta. To supply his force as it drove deeper and deeper into the enemy's country, Sherman relied upon a long, lonely railroad which, had the Southern horsemen been willing to work hard with their hands, might have been so badly crippled as to have compelled him to abandon his campaign. But as long as cavalrymen were cavalrymen, he was safe. His engineers traveling up and down the track could speedily repair all injuries.

So cynically did he hold the enemy cavalry that when word came that Wheeler was riding to destroy his source of supplies in Kentucky, Sherman sniffed, "I can't turn back for a cavalry raid. It is destined for clamor and nothing more."

Sherman's capture of Atlanta came when it did largely because General Wheeler had left the defending Southern army to stage a spread-eagle demonstration in the Union rear. It was expected that Sherman would relax his offensive to protect his line of supply, but "Uncle Billy" merely dispatched some infantry reserves to guard the larger supply depots and kept his army hammering at the Confederate defenses. With the Southern cavalry gone, Sherman seized the chance to ruin the railroad which fed Atlanta, and ordered his own head-horseman, Kilpatrick, to do the job. Emphatically, he lectured his centaur, "You go not to fight but to WORK." Soon little "Kil" was back with tall tales of how completely he had wrecked *that* road. But the next day, Sherman saw Confederate trains merrily running up and down the tracks as though nothing had happened and, in the end, the infantry had to fight its way around and perform the duty.

Although it is unquestionable that many of the Western Federal cavalry leaders were ferocious in battle, Sherman found difficulty in persuading several of them to fight consistently. Of General Hatch he once said, "I hear of no collision, of no killed. He seems to hover around when he should dash in with saber and pistol." And of another, General Garrad, he observed, "I am thoroughly convinced that, if he can see a horseman in the distance with a spy-glass, he will turn back."

It was Sherman's favorite assistant, General McPherson, however, who made the classic comment on this type of Union cavalrymen. McPherson was writing to Grant who had gone East to assume command of all the Northern armies. Since Grant was dismal at the time regarding the cavalry and was telling Lincoln that the service needed reformation, he was in a mood to appreciate McPherson's wire, which read, "There is no disguising the fact that the enemy cavalry brigades are far superior to ours under Winslow. Many of his [Winslow's] subordinate officers are of no account whatever; even the horses have caught the timidity of the men and turn around involuntarily and break for the rear as soon as a shot is fired."

Sherman had vexations, too, over General Sooy Smith who commanded his cavalry in the winter of 1863-64. The trouble came to a climax on an expedition wherein Smith, with the horsemen, was to meet Sherman, with the infantry, at Meridian, Mississippi, on a certain February day and wreck it. The foot soldiers arrived, but no Sooy. "It will be a novel thing in war if infantry has to await the motions of the cavalry," Sherman growled. At length the patient infantrymen, having reduced the city, returned home to find that Smith had poked along so leisurely that the enemy under Forrest had found time to organize a force of half his strength and whip him.

Similar disaster overtook all too many Union raids. General Kilpatrick and Colonel Dahlgren essayed a most sensational dash upon Richmond in February, 1864, but, beyond losing most of Dahlgren's riders and frightening the good folk of the Confederate capital into ringing the church bells in their nightshirts, accomplished nothing. Colonel Streight, in April, 1863, mounted 2,600 infantrymen on mules and set out to devastate northern Alabama. The bold party was gobbled up en masse by their enemies at Rome, Georgia. General Sturgis attempted a similar tour of northern Mississippi in May, 1864, and was captured, the catastrophe perhaps aided by the commander's enthusiasm for alcohol taken as a beverage. General Stoneman, weary of protecting Sherman's food lines in the Atlanta campaign, persuaded his superior to let him make a grand gesture. He would ride on Andersonville prison and free the thousands of piteous starvelings there. Sherman, swept off his balance by sympathy for the prisoners, allowed Stoneman to attempt it, but was not surprised to hear soon enough that the raiders, with outposts lulled by peach brandy and applejack, had been overwhelmed, and were themselves on the road to the prison pen.

To home populations, the very boldness and bravery of such pranks outweighed their lack of success. And as for the reputedly successful dashes of Wilder in Tennessee, Grierson and Stanley in Mississippi, their results were

never regarded by Sherman and McPherson as quite com-
mensurate with their celebrity.

Sherman's general contempt for cavalry was by no
means limited to his own force. For only one Confederate
horseman did he voice any respect. General Nathan Bed-
ford Forrest, that curious, unorthodox genius, drew compliments now and again from "Uncle Billy." Forrest as an
eccentric, non-military, subliterate individual, could never
learn the simplest commands nor manuals of arms, yet
he was, until the late months of the war, consistently victorious over the Yankee horsemen. As a slave-dealer Forrest had been beyond the social pale and was consequently
free from the technique of a gentleman. He merely used
common sense in thinking of his men as mounted infantry,
and he used horses primarily to move his riflemen from
one danger spot to another.

"That devil Forrest," Sherman sometimes called him,
and once was rumored to have said he would trade all his
own horsemen for Forrest alone. When Forrest's men
had massacred some Union troops, both colored and white,
after the flag of surrender had flown above Fort Pillow,
the whimsical genius became regarded as more or less of
an outlaw, and Sherman put a price on his head, offering
to make a major general out of any Union brigadier who
would kill Forrest in battle.

But examination of the record reveals that Sherman
paid Forrest a respect that was more conversational than
active. Forrest's elusiveness and incessant flouting of his
pursuers nettled Sherman and drew from him those ex-
plosive tributes. However much his tongue might run
away with him, Sherman had his hands always under
control. Tempted though he often was to send his re-

doubtable infantry against Forrest, he never did so when there was any need for them to be pounding the Confederate footmen who were serious enemies indeed. Forrest at his worst would only be defeating Union cavalry. And finally when the time was ripe, he sent his supermarchers, the troops of A. J. Smith and Mower to catch and crush Forrest.

When word would come, as it so often did, that Forrest was threatening his communications, Sherman would virtually yawn as he answered, "Let Forrest cavort about the country as much as he pleases."

For Joe Wheeler, the Southern cavalry-chief most often opposed to him, Sherman had small regard. Grant had written him, "Wheeler is easily whipped if boldly attacked by half his numbers," a description which Sherman found somewhat exaggerated yet true enough for all practical purposes. In his final campaign through the Carolinas, Sherman discovered that his own cavalry, under the cockerel Kilpatrick, was capable of pushing Wheeler back without serious interruption. Even when Wheeler would elude "Kil" and break through upon the infantry, there was still no cause for worry. "My marching columns of infantry don't pay the cavalry any attention, but walk right through it," Sherman wrote to Grant.

From the Official Records comes again and again the impression that Sherman, barring his occasional vexations over Forrest's impudence, was content to let the South have all the superiority in cavalry that it wanted.

Occasionally he would snap out some angry wish for better Union horsemen, but on second thought would register his more consistent belief that the more the Confederacy was encouraged to develop fiery and dashing bands of raiders, the better it was for the North. He saw that as the bands grew more and more independent, clattering far and wide, they naturally gravitated into lawlessness, and that while cavalrymen as a class might be plumed knights to distant newspaper readers, they were a plague to noncombatants near at hand.

Like all realists, he saw that the destruction of Chambersburg, Pennsylvania, by Confederate raiders, and the histrionic ride of John Morgan up through Indiana and Ohio had done nothing quite so much as convert droves of Southern sympathizers in these States into rabid Union men. Of the "secesh" cavalry organizations operating in Mississippi, Tennessee, and Alabama, he repeatedly said, "I don't want those rebel bands captured. They are doing us excellent service. They are disgusting the minds of the Southern people with Confederate pretension and government. I want the people to feel that their rebel authorities care but little for them."

As though to confirm his wisdom were the protests that Southern people made against their cavalry. Most succinct of these complaints was that of Sergeant L. G. Sleeper, 44th Mississippi Infantry, C. S. A., who on January 27, 1864, wrote the Southern Secretary of War, "The cavalry in southern Mississippi is a most perfect nuisance, a terror to the people and a disgrace to all civilized warfare. All men who are conscripted join this cavalry and consider themselves out of the service. I saw a number of absentees from this and other portions of our army who have deserted their commands and are actually protected by this cavalry."

Sheafs of demands that Wheeler's cavalry be curbed came to Richmond from the Georgians and Carolinians who had lost horses, quilts, corn, clothing, to their "protectors." In conversation, in letters, in newspapers and formal documents they declared that they saw no difference between the Union foragers and Wheeler's horsemen.

For much of this "horror" talk, the cavalryman's own habit of braggadocio was responsible. "We get the first whack at the women and the banks" was a jesting boast of riders who liked to impress listeners with their dare-deviltry. In reality their depredations in the Civil War did not include rape, a crime strikingly absent from the whole conflict.

Wheeler's dragoons, however, were so reckless with their friends' property as to draw official inquiry by the Confederate authorities, and of them Major General D. H. Hill, C. S. A., reported in January, 1864, "My experience with the cavalry in this war has not been favorable and I make no secret of my opinion. . . . There is something terribly wrong. They never think of delaying the Yankees by fighting them. Their simple business is to get out of the way. . . . What we need is efficient cavalry, not immense bands of plunderers scattered over the country. Nine-tenths of the so-called cavalry never see and cannot be induced to see an armed Yankee. If we are starved into submission, it will be through these fellows."

There may have been actual prophecy in Hill's words. Perhaps the Confederacy died prematurely from the effects of that enormous draught of Cavalierism which it drank so early in the war and which intoxicated it so gloriously.

To the end of the conflict the professional fire-eaters like Wade Hampton were orating, "Give me 20,000

cavalry and I'll drive Sherman out of the Carolinas."
Considering that Hampton had retired, with his cavalry,
from the sacred soil of South Carolina in February, 1865,
without giving Sherman any battles worth mentioning,
such bursts of bombast were only ridiculous.

Nevertheless, it was common for thirty years after the
war to find Southern cavalry-enthusiasts attacking Jefferson Davis for not having armed more horsemen during
the war. It was said that, if he had mounted great sections of the infantry and let the Southern aptitude for
horsemanship take its natural course, the Lost Cause would
never have been lost.

Well might Davis have answered—had he cared to take
up the matter—that the Confederacy suffered not from
too little cavalry but from too much.

Several brigades of those gay, cavorting Cavaliers, unhorsed and placed in the rifle pits, might have saved the
day at Gettysburg or Atlanta. The Confederate high
command at Richmond had, as early as December 23,
1863, been told the blunt truth by Lee's "war-horse,"
the realistic General Longstreet:

"I would respectfully suggest that we have already
more cavalry than we need, and not enough of infantry.
Besides, our country [eastern Tennessee, western North
Carolina, northern Georgia, and southwestern Virginia]
is completely overrun by cavalry; farms destroyed and
forage and subsistence consumed and wasted to such an
extent that I am apprehensive that we shall not be able to
get along. Partisan cavalry, having authority to keep and
sell everything that they capture, do not always confine
their captures to the enemy's side. Horses, mules, cattle,
and, in some instances, Negroes are taken and sent south

and sold. The other cavalry [regular Confederate] seems to have taken up the idea that they should enjoy like privileges, and frequently take property captured from the enemy and from our own citizens and dispose of it to their own advantage.

"I fear that this feeling to acquire property is more at heart with much of our cavalry than a disposition to drive the enemy from our soil.

"I would suggest, therefore, that all partisan cavalry be made regular cavalry by law, if they so elect. Failing in this choice, it would be well to disband all such organizations and let the men be subject to conscription. . . . I would also suggest that no other soldiers be enlisted in the cavalry."

While the real life of cavalry as a vital arm of modern warfare may be said to have died with the Confederacy, it was a Union horseman who signaled its interment—a Federal cavalryman who was as brimming with cavalier romance as any Jeb Stuart.

The tragedy occurred on the twenty-second of May, 1865, when the Union Army of the Potomac held its grand review to celebrate victory in Washington. Pennsylvania Avenue was swarming with a throng even larger than it had held a month before when Lincoln's funeral had rolled on black wheels from the White House to the Capitol. Crowds screamed, banners flew, dignitaries craned their necks, little boys fell out of shade trees from sheer excitement. The soldiers were starched and polished almost beyond endurance and the most gorgeous figure of all was Major General George Armstrong Custer, whose velveteen uniform was the bluest of blues and whose long yellow hair floated in the wind—the same long, yellow hair that would later dangle from Indian belts on the plains where cavalry would flourish for a time in a revival of primitive, savage warfare.

Behind Custer rode the dragoons who had followed him in Sheridan's Shenandoah campaign. No other horsemen were so spangled and so fancy as Custer's men, each man with a long scarf, a paper collar, and a pink ribbon around his neck.

Bands blared, the horses quivered, and the parade began. All eyes were on "Yellow Hair"—who had been a brigadier general at twenty-four—the man who would demonstrate to the world how the cavalry—that fairest flower of chivalry—could ride.

Suddenly in the crowd an overwrought female threw a wreath of blossoms at Custer's head. The missile fell short and settled over the eyes of Custer's horse. A snort, and away went the frightened charger, the bit between its teeth, soldiers, civilians scrambling, and the poor general hanging on for dear life. He disappeared in the distance and the parade went off without him.

A Dreamlike Concern

Verbatim transcript of the remarks of Tom Blevins (see page 3) made to me in a cabin at Cockleburr Springs, thirty-five miles in the desert from Jensen, Utah. This took place on the night of October 31, 1924.

WELL, Lloyd, if you feel anyways funny, I'll tell you about "The Two Minnies." That was the finest place a cowboy could be and most talked of, I reckon, around the wagons at night all through Texas and the Territory. Lots of time a feller would be singin' "Rock of Ages" to quiet the cattle and thinkin' about "The Two Minnies."

Outside, it was just like any big block, and when the two Minnies come to Fort Worth in 1873 and put it up in what they called "Hell's Half Acre," it was about the biggest show place in town fer size. Pretty soon that part of town got to be hell's whole acre, but the first time I seen it, it was smallish and all anybody talked about was "The Two Minnies."

I seen it first in 1874. I had got back from drivin' John Chisholm's cattle to the railroad and John says, "Tom, take a rest. You've been workin' steady fer two years and a foreman gets wore out. Here's four months' wages. Ride over to Fort Worth and get rollicky a spell." And he says, "You've never seen 'The Two Minnies,' have you?"

None of the common cowpunchers knowed about it then. Later on, when the word got spread all over Texas and the Territory, a man would know what to expect, but then nobody did, so I just walked in and seen a hell of a big, fine room with cushion chairs and tables to drink off of all in front of the bar. I'd been ridin' three days and I made a line for the bar, but a big nigger stopped me and took my chaps and my gun so polite and hung 'em up.

I ast fer whiskey and wanted to set 'em up fer the house, but the bartender frowned and drawed himself up. "The Two Minnies" had the dudiest-lookin' men they could git, pins that shone, and had their hair combed. So I poured out a drink and said to myself, "Don't look like you're goin' to have much fun here," and throwed back my head fer to swallow it—but I never got that drink. No man ever got his first drink in "The Two Minnies" —fer the ceilin' was glass and there was anyways forty chippies walkin' around up there naked playin' tenpins.

They was as fine a-lookin' women as you'd ever want fer to see—laughin' quiet to themselves and they'd take their turns to bowl and start their roll, but the alley wasn't on the glass. It was off to one side.

I set down in one of them big lather chairs with another man and then I could take in the whole room upstairs better.

Them women lived up there. Some of 'em was sewin' and some readin' and some playin' guitars and niggers in shimmy-soled shoes was washin' and polishin' the glass floor when I got there.

Once in a while one of the women would look down into the barroom and kind of smile and then go on talkin' with the other girls. Around the edge they had long sofeys and a thousand lamps. It was about as light as the plains before it gets dark.

They was all plumb stark naked. They seemed like that

was the way they'd been born and had never knowed there was clothes in the world—or anyways had thought that clothes was just fer men.

There was no women down in the barroom and had never been any. The girls up there was never allowed to come down and no woman from the outside was allowed to come in. First time in my life I ever seen a bartender too high-toned to wait on a chippy.

Them niggers in their shoes with them shimmy-skin soles would bring them women up there their meals, and they'd eat with fine manners and wipe their mouths with napkins—I guess of silk anyway—and they'd drink wine out of long glasses and the niggers waited on 'em careful and quiet and hauled stuff up on dumb-waiters fer 'em.

All you could hear downstairs was when them girls would laugh sometimes, or play the guitar, or do a little singin'.

It was a kind of a dreamlike concern.

There was velvet curtains all around the room and the fellow in the chair beside me said that the girls' rooms was behind there somewhere.

"You've got to be dressed up to get up there," he says. He was a rich buffalo-skinner and had knowed the place fer a year or more, he said. "There's a regular price fer certain hours," he says. "Five dollars up to ten o'clock at night and then ten dollars from then to morning. You have to get a ticket at the bar and go up them stairs back there, and as soon as you open that door, there's a big feller in striped pants all dressed up like Prince Albert and he takes your ticket.

"The girls get half the five dollars and six of the ten dollars and their board—they don't need no clothes from the time they come here till they go—and ten per cent of the drinks served in the bar down here and their license paid. Then they get to keep half of what's stole. Poor innocent chippies wouldn't turn all that in, I guess.

"I've known a girl to lift $1,000 off one of these big cotton men that comes up here from Mississippi by the trainload, and ruther than fer his family to know, he'd keep still about it."

I told the man it was funny to me, fer they didn't seem like the girls I'd knowed in them rough-and-tumble parlor houses back at St. Angelo and Wichita Falls and Eddy—that's named Carlosbad now.

"Oh, no," the buffalo feller says, "there's none of them green sagebrush girls here; they're all from New York and Paris and have got educations. I'll say that fer 'em; they're just as fine a-talkin' women as you'll ever find anywheres," he says.

Along about four o'clock that afternoon the two Minnies come in. They was the owners and full sisters and wore Paris styles and had drove up in an open carriage with niggers to drive and watch out behind and to open the doors and spread dusters over their laps. The two Minnies was smart women. They was French and there was six sisters of 'em all together, the other four run "The Four Minnies" in Mexico City, just like this "Two Minnies" place in Fort Worth with the same glass ceilin' business, but they had more girls—sixty of 'em anyways, livin' up there. The Minnies would visit back and forth some but they all stuck to business close. They was in it fer the money, and the buffalo man—he introduced me to the youngest one of the two Minnies, Little Minnie, and she said, "The minute this place begins to run behind, we quit."

They come in with their bookkeepers, slick-lookin' men who went right to the cash drawers and checked up on the bartenders and on the ticket man in the striped pants and put the money in satchels and went out with the two Minnies. Then a new shift of bartenders come on and the girls had their supper with the niggers hurryin'.

"Them two Minnies, they never have anything to do with men that come here," the buffalo feller told me. "They're too rich," he says. "They live with them bookkeepers. They've got a big, fine mansion up on Tucker's Hill, and you'll only see 'em like you did now drive up with fast-trottin' horses and get the money. This place here is worth a hundred thousand dollars and these pictures that's on the walls, they brought over from France."

Well, along in the evening about midnight I come back from supper and seein' to my horse down in the feedbarn and everything was changed. You had to ring a bell to get in and a nigger looked you over.

At night a man wasn't allowed on the glass floor unless he was naked, too. He got more attention paid him, more of the niggers would run to get him wine. It was $16 a quart and a ticket to get up cost $10. More of the girls would run to git him a match, or a glass, or to play him a tune, or insist on him dancin'. They had an orchestra of niggers playin' Mexican waltzes.

They was rollicky but not rough this time of night. They'd just dance and laugh and drink and get old men to bettin' on a game of tenpins. It was a plumb silly sight to see some old cowman dancin' with a ring of women around him.

It was no place fer a cowboy. He could have more fun in them sagebrush houses and not have to worry about style. The two Minnies didn't like cowboys on the glass floor, fer a cowboy would shoot up the place fer $15 stole off him, while these rich cowmen and buffalo skinners and cotton men would keep still.

The two Minnies stayed fer eight years till the railroads shipped all the buffalo hides out of the country, then they went away. I was in there a hundred times, I reckon, but there was never no real fun in "The Two Minnies," no yellin', and we could have more fun over at St. Angelo's in Frankie Day's place.

Last of the Troubadours*

THE best singing Carl Sandburg ever did was at the dinner Morris Fishbein gave for Sinclair Lewis in 1925. Lewis had just come back from England, and Fishbein had assembled the local authors and critics to meet him— a score of guests or so—quite an affair.

Everybody but the distinguished guest was talking about the British baronetcy that Lewis had turned down, and Ben Hecht got to calling him "Sir Red" on account of that and his red hair. To add to the whoop-de-doodle, James Weber Linn, the University of Chicago English professor, got himself jumped on by Lewis for some things he had said about *Main Street*, and Hecht immediately sided with "Sir Red" and attacked Linn on the flank. Some of the other young rebels joined in, accusing Linn of conservatism in literature, and for a good hour Professor Weber was a verbal Doug Fairbanks, fencing with a dozen swordsmen all at once on a narrow stair, and doing a gallant job of it, too. The hullabaloo grew general.

Down at the very end of the table, opposite the host, sat Chicago's biggest literary figure, Carl Sandburg, behind his hair and his stogy. Every once in a while Carl would shoot in a remark like a Virginia sharpshooter in leather pants, stepping out from behind a hickory tree to plug a Tory, then stepping back to load his muzzle-loader again.

* Copyright 1929 by *The Chicagoan*.

At length Fishbein, to keep his tablecloth from being bitten, asked Carl if he'd sing. Somebody brought a guitar and the iron-jawed Swede stood up and, in that soft, don't-give-a-damn way of his, sang "The Buffalo Skinners."

Everything got quiet as a church, for it's a great rough song, all about starvation, blood, fleas, hides, entrails, thirst, and Indian-devils, and men being cheated out of their wages and killing their employers to get even—a novel, an epic novel boiled down to simple words and set to queer music that rises and falls like the winds on Western plains. I've heard the discoverer of the song, John Lomax, of Texas, sing it, but never like Carl sang it this night. It was like a funeral song to the pioneer America that has gone, and when Carl was done Sinclair Lewis spoke up, his face streaked with tears, "That's the America I came home to. That's it."

Most of the other guests were swallowing hard, too, and everybody was sort of glad when Keith Preston, the Chicago *Daily News* columnist and wit, piped up to break the spell. Keith nodded his head at Lewis and said, "Kind hearts are more than coronets."

They all laughed at that—Lewis, too—and Sandburg went on to livelier songs. It was the first time a lot of supposedly well-informed men knew Carl as anything but a poet and newspaperman. As a matter of fact, he'd been singing for eight or nine years on the platform from coast to coast, filling all the engagements he could handle, and at the time he was busy with engagements that netted him $250 a throw and all expenses. Later on he published his *American Songbag* and all the writers and critics knew about his singing, but to this day few of them seem to realize that the man is at his greatest with a guitar in his hand—undeniably a complete and independent artist.

Sandburg may not be a great singer, but his singing is great. That night, leaving Fishbein's, Harry Hansen kept saying, "He's a great, great artist," and somebody said, "Who, Lewis?" and Hansen said, "Sandburg! Sinclair Lewis is great, too, of course, but Sandburg can sing." But even Harry never wrote about Carl's singing as he did about Carl's poetry and prose. Neither has anybody else. I could never understand why not.

The man's voice is heavy and untrained—he has never had but three vocal lessons and they were from a choir singer in Galesburg, Illinois, long ago—and all his accomplishments on the guitar sound alike, but from every song that he sings there comes a mood, a character, an emotion. He just stands there, swaying a little like a tree, and sings, and you see farmhands wailing their lonely ballads, hillbillies lamenting over drowned girls, levee hands in the throes of the blues, cowboys singing down their herds, barroom loafers howling for sweeter women, Irish section hands wanting to go home, hoboes making fun of Jay Gould's daughter. The characters are real as life, only more lyric than life ever quite gets to be.

Some of the book reviewers halfway regret Sandburg's career as a platform singer, wishing that he'd spend the time writing. What they don't understand is that the man earns a happy livelihood at this art so that he can write exactly what he wants to write when he sits down to write.

All kinds of people engage him to come and read his poetry and sing to them—college students, Gold Coast society, labor unions, school teachers' institutes, Harvard University Phi Beta Kappa conventions, radicals and Republican clubs alike, editors' conventions. Twice Broadway revues have tempted him, but both times he has answered, "The best things in song that I've got have been with my back to Broadway. I admire Irving Berlin as a business-man, but as an artist he's a master song-plugger. To hell with Tin Pan Alley."

As a workman, Sandburg has more in common with Grover Cleveland Alexander than with Al Jolson. He sings like Alexander pitches baseball—cool and slow. He stands long looking at an audience like Alex the Great looks at a batter. Both men are gray and cunning, easy and spare of style. It is characteristic of Carl that he re-sembles the pitcher. In Lombard College, Carl had base-ball ambitions and, without the necessity of earning his tuition by delivering milk, might have become the pro-fessional outfielder that he wanted to be. Diamond slang crops out in his speech all the time, as when he instructs his agents never to book him for two consecutive lectures. "I can't pitch two games in a row," he says.

Many listeners have asked him to teach them his vocal method. Always he eludes them in his slow, knowing way, understanding well enough that his method is not so much a method as a philosophy of life, a solitary art evolved in loneliness and in an eternal faith in democracy.

Public singing had started for Sandburg about thirteen years before. Up to that time he had been piling up ex-perience. Born in Galesburg to a Swedish immigrant and his wife—a stout, vital pair, at home in the new prairies—Carl had worked his way through college, sleeping in a bitter, unheated room in winter, a strange scholar going his own way, avoiding the college glee club but singing with barber-shop harmonizers downtown, reading books with his own eyes, not those of his teachers. He graduated, but not until he had served in the Spanish-American War, traveled over the country "hooking rides" on freight trains, avoiding town-marshals narrowly—once unsuccessfully—working his way, the sort of Swede boy in whom the Viking blood was always fermenting. To this day Sandburg likes to be free to go. He is most indefinite about his comings and goings, although not when lecture engagements are to be kept.

As a youth he roamed, worked, and cogitated. Socialism drew him. From boyhood he had written odd little things down on paper and had either thrown or tucked them away. In Milwaukee, where he was the secretary of a Socialistic mayor, he took to expressing himself on the stump. In Lombard College he had won the Swan Declamation Prize. For Union Labor he stumped widely, wrote arguments, campaigned for and among the workers. In this period he wrote the poetic denunciation of the Reverend Billy Sunday that, to this day, remains as the most thorough skinning that the evangelist ever received.

When *The Day Book*, an adless newspaper for the masses, was started in Chicago, Sandburg was a staff writer. The salary, $27.50 a week, was less than other newspapers would have paid him, but it was work he wanted to do. He ate sparingly, rode the street cars as far as they went toward Maywood, his home, then walked the rest of the way. In one-arm lunchrooms and on the trolleys he wrote poems; walking under the stars, he thought about other poems. *Poetry Magazine* began printing them, gave him a prize; a New York publisher issued them. Book pages across the country showed the impact the volume *Chicago Poems* had caused. He rose up along-

side Edgar Lee Masters and Vachel Lindsay and Sherwood Anderson.

However, to get back to the plain facts of Sandburgiana,
The Day Book failed during the war. Sandburg, the
Spanish-American veteran, mooned around looking at
flags and guns, listening to old calls. But he had a wife
and three children now and the Viking blood had to cool.
He worked for the Newspaper Enterprise Association,
and then for the *Chicago Daily News*, where he remained,
as reporter, then movie critic, and later as bi-weekly
columnist.

But with the fame of being a poet back in 1916, he
began to get calls to a new business, that of lecturing.
"Come and read your poems," he was told. At the end
of one of these very first readings, he laid aside *Chicago
Poems*, dug out a guitar from behind the rostrum, and
said, "I will now sing a few folk-songs that somehow tie
into the folk-quality I have tried to get into my verse.
They are all authentic songs people have sung for years.
If you don't care for them and want to leave the hall, it
will be all right with me. I'll only be doing what I'd be
doing if I were home, anyway."

The audience stayed, liking the songs better than the
poems, and since that day the singing has been half of
every program. When the Republican Club of New York
asked him, as the author of *Abraham Lincoln: The Prairie
Years*, to address it, they added, "Bring along your
guitar."

All through his roamings as a youth Sandburg listened
to the songs people sang. He jotted them down, using a
weird system of musical shorthand. And as he went about

the country, in this later period of his career giving song-lectures, new folk-songs rolled in on him.

There is nothing dearer to the average person than to give great people assistance. Sandburg reaped this harvest. Lecture-committees in towns where he came to read and sing soon learned that Sandburg is one of the de luxe guests of Our Times. Picturesque in his long, prematurely gray hair, his speech and his gentle roughness, he colors up a living room immoderately. When he feels at home, he will sing, tell anecdotes in tantalizing slowness, and make his hosts ecstatic. With such ability he has found himself, for years, swamped with proffers of folk-songs. Traveling as he has all over America, he had the chance to winnow out the best from a colossal number of songs. Of these he made *The American Songbag* of 300-odd selections. This, published in 1927, was his eighth book.

Chicago Poems (1915), *Cornhuskers* (1918), *Smoke and Steel* (1920), *Slabs of the Sunburnt West* (1923), *Rootabaga Stories* (1922), *Rootabaga Pigeons* (1923), *Abraham Lincoln: The Prairie Years* (1926), have been the others. Only *Lincoln* is straight prose. The Rootabaga books are prose poems, midland fairy tales for children, replacements for kings and elves offered in the form of familiar prairie words and objects.

From his home he goes out no more than twenty-five times a year to read his poems and sing his songs. For one thing, he is free from money worries. The magazine serial rights on *Lincoln* alone were a young fortune. For another thing, he is deep in other books—and he likes to swim and play with his kids. His Viking blood can find outlets now on printed pages instead of on the blinds of express trains heading West.

"I can't be hurried," is his favorite saying, as he jogs off in his bathing pants to run down the beach and swim for an hour.

A slow change has come over his songs of late years— fewer and fewer have become hobo songs on his programs. Scarcely ever nowadays does he include the I.W.W. marching song:

> Oh why don't you work like other men do?
> How the hell can I work when there's no work to do?
> Hallelujah! I'm a bum.
> Hallelujah! Bum again.
> Hallelujah! Give us a hand-out
> To revive us again.

He still uses a dehorned version of "Frankie and Johnny" to grand effect, but imaginative, fantastic Negro spirituals occupy a larger place on his programs now. Sandburg has become quieter, deeper, more spiritual, better tuned to the abstract pathos of song. He no longer strains at the last line for emphasis.

As the years enrich his collection of folk-songs he becomes more secure in his conviction that the common people are instinctively better artists than the pontifical experts will admit.

"Culture," he once said, "is the product of many minds. A song that has grown slowly, passing from mouth to mouth, is apt to acquire a dignity and an endurance that a composition by one man will not possess. As a boy, I was suspicious of vocal training and I stayed away from the college glee club, yet I've missed few chances to hear great singers. I learned from them to sing with the whole body and to make every song a role."

He is the last of the troubadours, is Sandburg, the last

of the nomad artists who hunted out the songs people made up, and then sang them back to the people like a revelation. An American Ossian, a throwback to the days when songs passed from mouth to mouth. Both his singing and his search for songs are part of his belief in the essential merit of the common man. Like Whitman, his philosophy is that of a pioneer Quaker who has turned paradoxically to song. Rousseau, Goethe, and old Walt would have sat up at night to hear him sing. George Fox, for all his Quaker distrust of music, would have understood him perfectly.

However, that is speculation. All I know for sure is that you should have heard him sing the night he made Sinclair Lewis cry.

The Holy Spirit at West Point

THE Word of God came to the United States Military Academy in 1825, the twenty-third year of its existence, on a certain winter morning. It arrived with a spiritual detonation as thunderous as if one of the campus cannon had suddenly fired off and kicked itself over the cliffs into the Hudson.

Chaplain Charles Pettit McIlvaine, a majestic Episcopalian, was on the rostrum that morning conducting chapel exercises. The cadets huddled before him on backless benches that were so crowded that one boy's knees fit into another boy's back. Ever since his arrival at the Academy early in the year, Dr. McIlvaine had seen the cadets sitting thus, unresponsive, almost defiant. "The condition of the Academy was far from encouraging," he recalled in later years. "There was not one 'professor of religion' among the officers. Of the cadets not one was known to make any profession of interest. Among cadets, officers, and instructors there was a great deal of avowed infidelity."

This attitude, at the time, had become traditional in the United States Army. Since the Revolution the bulk of American professional soldiers, like the leading American statesmen, had been skeptical of organized religion. Intimacy with French guest-officers in the struggle for Independence had spread Voltaire's Deism, and Thomas

Jefferson had used his immense influence to weaken the power of orthodox Christianity.

But on this particular morning at West Point, Dr. McIlvaine got unexpected encouragement when, during that portion of the Episcopal service which deals with the confession, the chapel resounded with a scraping, scuffling noise. A cadet was shoving benches about and moving neighboring feet so that he might have room to kneel! Jaws dropped open in amazement as the youth spoke his responses in a trembling voice. Nothing like this had ever happened before.

But over among the first-year men there was a stripling Virginian who knew quite well what the kneeling cadet was doing. Robert E. Lee, at eighteen, was already a devout Christian, even if as a plebe he kept himself so inconspicuous that Chaplain McIlvaine was not yet aware of him. He neither swore, drank, nor used tobacco, and never did anything that he couldn't tell his mother. Near by sat his friend and classmate, Joseph E. Johnston, a youngster of no religion. Yet forty years hence Johnston would be kneeling on the battlefield for baptism at the hands of the same cadet at whom the whole student body was now staring.

Soon it was made out that the convert was Leonidas Polk, a tall North Carolinian who had heretofore been ready and capable in mischief. As a third-year man and roommate of the popular fourth-year cadet, Albert Sydney Johnston, young Polk was a rare prize for Dr. McIlvaine. None of the boys dared ridicule so influential a person. Back home in North Carolina, his father, a hard-headed old colonel of Revolutionary days, would object to his son's conversion, but it would do no good. Leonidas had

taken Christ to his bosom for good and all, and within a
week would be inducing other cadets to kneel in chapel
and shepherding them into prayer-meetings which the
eloquent McIlvaine held nightly in various rooms.

Leonidas, indeed, became so extremely pious that he
was soon allowing himself to be used by the commandant
as an instrument of discipline in the school. It seems that
the august fourth-year men had for years refused to
answer roll-call in the morning. None of the lower class-
men dared offend their seniors by rousting them out of
bed. But with the Holy Spirit in his heart, Leonidas was
now on the side of authority and did the commandant's
bidding, tossing his superiors out on the cold floor in their
nightshirts.

Religion was so strong in him and brought him such
sweet glimpses of righteous power that he resigned from
the army soon after graduation and became a priest of
the Protestant Episcopal Church. By 1838 he was Bishop
of Louisiana, Texas, and the Indian Territory. Dr. Mc-
Ilvaine, too, soon left the Academy, to embark upon a
church career that was to make him Bishop of Ohio in
1832.

The revival that the two launched at West Point per-
manently rescued the place from agnosticism. It became
Christian, so much so that, in time, its critics would be
sneering, "It's a great place to make preachers." Its
friends, too, were to remark how many clergymen were
educated there. Roswell Park, leader of the class of 1831,
left the army to become an Episcopalian dominie and
educator, and others of less celebrity found it easy to step
from the profession of war to that of orthodox religion.
Both disciplines, as taught at West Point, were strict and

firm of rule; each bent the will of man to higher authority. Duty and obedience were the watchwords of both militarism and Calvinism.

Between 1825 and 1861 the West Pointers were thus grounded in a firm trust in things-as-they-are. The codes of church, state, and society were to be supported as established. The Academy schooled reactionary, aristocratic conformists, who distrusted the free play of politicians' minds and political agitation in general. As a group they regarded slavery as a sacred institution, for it had always been here. Antislavery workers they scorned as sinful anarchists. With the South dominating the Academy, as it did the whole government, the boys did not question the superiority of the slaveholding aristocracy. In the years between its organization in 1802 and the national crisis of 1861, West Point had had one cadet for every 5,757 persons in the South and only one for every 8,330 Northerners. Even those Northern cadets who believed Secession wrong were apt to class Abolition as no better.

George B. McClellan, the little New Yorker who graduated in 1846, regarded the agitators of Massachusetts and South Carolina as equally to blame for the Civil War when it came, and was said to have wished that someone would heave both States into the ocean. McClellan was quite typical of the West Pointers of his day. In faith he was a Presbyterian Fundamentalist and in politics, a conservative. In war he would always play safe, and be strong on the defensive, weak and uninventive in attack, true to the Academy teachings.

It was upon men like McClellan that President Lincoln had to rely when war came in 1861—bureaucrats and classic tacticians who had no desire either to use Southern people harshly or to destroy slavery. As near as one can get at their common aim, it was to end the war by brilliant maneuvers and re-establish the Union with slavery intact. Their minds, narrowed by their training in orthodoxy, could grasp the mass passions of neither population, North or South, and all of them were awed by the fact that many of their old schoolmasters were high in the Confederate councils.

II

Between 1852 and 1860 West Point had been under the influence of two Episcopalians who would later become Confederate generals; Robert E. Lee was Superintendent of the Academy from 1852 to 1855 and William J. Hardee was Commandant of Cadets from 1856 to 1860. Furthermore, Jefferson Davis, President of the Confederacy, was an old West Pointer, and as Secretary of War from 1853 to 1857 had seemed almost like Jehovah Himself to the cadets. Numerous other Southern officers had served on the Academy faculty, and so, all in all, many of the Union war-leaders in the 'Sixties felt like schoolboys again.

Both Lee and Hardee were unquestioning in religion, and although their administrations raised the educational standards at the Academy, they kept the place studiously orthodox. Lee's essential conservatism was in evidence later, when, as a commander in the field, he was perfect on defense yet failed whenever he essayed big, bold movements into the enemy's territory. Also, he was so unprogressive as to oppose the introduction of the new breech-loading rifles which the Northerners had taken up with such deadly effect.

It is significant that of the three graduates who were in the war to be most elastic, inventive, and successful in mastering the business of attack, none was considered a star at West Point. Grant, Sherman, and Stonewall Jackson all left the Army in discouragement, Grant and Sherman to find failure in civil life and Jackson to become an indifferent school teacher. Each of them refused to abide by precedent when he found himself face to face with actual war. Grant introduced the innovation of refusing to regard single battles as important; he ignored the formality of resting after a fight and astounded the classical tacticians by paying no attention to defeats, doggedly lunging ahead on a continuous campaign that eventually broke down all opposition. Sherman was equally unorthodox and independent, violating, with repeated success, the old West Point teaching, "Never divide your forces in the face of the enemy." And both Jackson and Sherman developed the artistry of forced marching to a degree which baffled their conservative adversaries.

Of the three men, Jackson alone was religious. Grant, at West Point and afterward, remained passive toward the Methodism of his mother. Sherman always declared himself "nothing in religion," although, as a nine-year-old boy, he had been baptized, at his foster-mother's insistence, into the Roman Catholic church. Jackson was a zealous Presbyterian, fond of establishing Sunday schools for slaves. As a wartime leader, he looked to many men like nothing so much as a brooding, circuit-riding Methodist preacher, shambling along with his feet out of the stirrups, as slouchy and unconventional in dress as Grant and Sherman. Born poor, living humbly, he was as far from the formalism of West Point as were either of the two Northerners with whom he had so much in common. Shot down, while serving as Lee's right arm, he disappeared from the war so early that one can only speculate as to the place he would have held at its end.

The Confederate Army of Northern Virginia, under Lee and Jackson, was notable for its hearty prayers. Indeed, the Southern forces from the first were more given to religious exercises than the Northern troops—a circumstance often explained by ascribing it to the influence of Lee. As partial substantiation for this belief, there is the fact that an unusual number of cadets were avowed Christians while Lee was commandant at West Point. Four of them later became Northern generals—Charles G. Harker, a Union brigadier who read the Bible in his tent every night; William Sooy Smith, the Western cavalry leader; James Birdseye McPherson, the favorite of Grant and Sherman, and O. O. Howard, who would fight Confederates in nine States, and Indians across the Wild West, lose an arm—yet remain famous through it all as the "Christian Soldier."

Howard's piety made him the butt of those cadets who disliked any excessive zeal for Bible classes. As one of the few youths at West Point to champion antislaveryism, Howard made himself obnoxious to the Southern students and had to defend himself with his fists. Always a militant fellow, he recalled, in later years, his pride in finding that Sooy Smith and McPherson would, even in their plebe years, before Lee's Christianizing influence arrived, stand up with him to profess Christianity.

How long McPherson's Calvinism lasted is open to question. As the leader of his class and the most popular cadet of his generation, he was a marked man and, as a

leader under Sherman, he was adored by the Western
Army—facts which brought his whole life into exhaustive
review when in 1864 he fell dramatically in battle. None
of his many eulogists, outside of Howard, remembered
anything more about his religion than that his character
had been singularly pure. His popularity with the Western
Army does not argue that he was conspicuously pious in
adult life, for the Army of the Tennessee, which he commanded, was notoriously free-thinking, the wildest and
most roistering of all the American forces. Its men loved
McPherson for his joviality, and the G.A.R. veterans of
later years used to chuckle as they recalled how the handsome Mac—a major general at thirty-five—had sung
serenades under the windows of the Vicksburg belles.

Howard, who came West to join Sherman at the start
of the Atlanta campaign, was ridiculed by the men for his
insistence that they stop swearing and drinking, and Carl
Schurz declared that Sherman shared their view of him.
Once, in Tennessee, Schurz was sitting in Sherman's field
headquarters with several generals awaiting breakfast.
Howard, passing by, saw blue smoke arising and came in
rubbing his hands, for it was frosty outside.

Sherman, speaking up in his brusque, short manner,
snapped, "Glad to see you, Howard. Sit down by the fire.
Damned cold this morning."

Howard, who abhorred even this mild type of swearing,
answered demurely, "Yes, General, it is *quite* cold this
morning."

At this Sherman shot a derisive grimace and a large
wink at General Jefferson C. Davis, the Hoosier professional soldier, who slouched in a near-by chair. Davis
was notoriously the most profane man in the Western

Army, a fiery fellow, fresh, at the time, from the shooting of a brother general who had insulted him in a Louisville hotel. Catching Sherman's signal, Davis leaned back and launched upon a trivial theme which gave him opportunity to disgorge the most fiendish oaths he could remember. Poor Howard tried weakly to turn the subject, but Davis, encouraged by winks and sympathetic remarks from Sherman, climbed higher and higher on the ladder of his art until the Christian General, with distress dripping from his face, fled without waiting for breakfast. As the door slammed, Sherman and Davis burst into roars of laughter.

Tenderhearted Schurz remonstrated, but Sherman cut him short. "That Christian Soldier business is all right in its place, but he needn't put on airs when we are among ourselves."

Howard, for all his piety, was a courageous fighter, as the empty sleeve pinned to his right breast testified, and Schurz rejoiced a little later when Sherman officially praised him "as one who mingles so gracefully and perfectly the polished Christian officer and the prompt, zealous, and gallant soldier."

After graduating from West Point in 1854, Howard remained on the faculty until 1861, teaching mathematics and Sunday school. Thus, he came to the field with the notion that it was wrong to have military maneuvers on the Sabbath. This idea was common among the Academy graduates of his generation. At the Battle of Bull Run, he heard officers say, "It is Sunday. The attacking party on the Sabbath is sure of defeat." Howard quoted this often and, when he had his way, kept the men in camp on the Lord's Day, while he himself took fruit to the hospitals and sang hymns with the wounded soldiers.

William S. Rosecrans, of the class of 1842, shared this prejudice against Sunday fighting, although it is doubtful if, after the Battle of Chickamauga, he continued to believe that the attacking party was sure of defeat. The Confederates fell upon him there on a Sunday and whipped him soundly. During the battle, Charles A. Dana, Assistant Secretary of War, thinking the day secure, took a nap in Rosecrans' tent and awoke to find the army in flight and Rosecrans crossing himself in prayer.

Rosecrans was, indeed, almost as much of a preacher by nature as his brother Sylvester, whom he persuaded to join him in his conversion to Roman Catholicism. Sylvester became a famous priest of Cincinnati, and William's habit was to lecture and preach to his men as he rode among them. Fresh from Mass each morning, the General would ride slowly through the camp, his red face beaming with kindliness, saying over and over, "Eat well, sleep well, keep well."

In battle he would not remain in lofty thought like so many West Point generals, but would go up and down the lines urging the soldiers to "Aim low! Aim low!" In sharp distinction to this fatherly practice was the method employed by certain rougher and readier officers who had come into the service from civil life. Some of them would race up and down behind the lines, swearing wildly and whacking the posteriors of the crouching riflemen with their big slouch hats.

It was said that Lee and Jackson also disliked to fight on Sunday, although they were known to do so when it seemed wise from a military standpoint. McClellan, as general-in-chief of the Union Armies, declared, "One day's rest in seven is necessary to men and animals. More than this, the observance of the holy day of the Lord God of mercy and of battles is our sacred duty."

Howard nettled Sherman most by his enthusiasm for importing members of the Christian Commission into the field during busy campaigns. Sherman, who expelled them whenever he found them in the way, had a realistic concept of his job, and objected to carrying such people on trains when the space was needed to bring up oats to feed the Army mules.

Once a protégé of Howard's on the Christian Commission, the Reverend E. P. Smith, took advantage of a lull in the daily battles to prepare an abandoned church for service. It was Sunday and a very good time to remind the Western Army of God, since Sherman paid no attention to the Sabbath.

All alone in the church, Preacher Smith climbed into the belfry to adjust the bell-rope, got caught somehow, and ripped the seat from his trousers. In his hurried descent he jangled the bell and so disturbed Sherman who, in a near-by cottage, was wrapt in his military plans. Abstractedly, Sherman ordered someone to see who was ringing the bell and a squad of soldiers arrived to find the wretched cleric trying to survey the ruin in his rear.

"Come along; the General wants you."

"I can't go like this. Take me where I can get fixed up first."

"Them's not the orders. Fall in!"

An aide brought the horrified dominie up to Sherman, saying, "Here's the man who was ringing that bell. He says it's Sunday—"

Sherman looked up, repeating in puzzlement, "Sunday? Sunday? Oh, yes, *Sunday!* Didn't know it was Sunday. Let him go—let him go."

Under such a chieftain as Sherman and commanding such troops as the Western squirrel-riflemen, Howard must have often wished that he was back with the more conventional Eastern Armies, with which he had served the first two years of the war. War was more of a gentleman's game there.

Like that other West Pointer, the solemn and immaculate George B. Thomas, who had been Sherman's classmate and friend at the Point and who now commanded one of his wings, Howard wondered at the responsibility which the chief gave to volunteer officers—mainly politicians such as John A. Logan of Illinois, Frank Blair of Missouri, John M. Palmer of Illinois, Alpheus Williams of Detroit, and John W. Geary, *alcalde* of San Francisco.

Sherman himself disliked the frequency with which Logan and Blair went home to deliver political speeches, but he understood very clearly why Lincoln had, at the outset of the war, given high military rank to politicians in sections of the country where pro-Union sentiment was doubtful. The volunteer generals in the Atlanta campaign were the best of their lot, winnowed out by years of fighting. The West Pointers in their paper collars might criticize the imperfect discipline and faulty tactics of these citizen-commanders, but they could not object to the results of their fighting. As combat leaders, Logan and his volunteer class were superb. They knew better than the West Pointers how to fire Western plowboys to desperate action. The troops felt at home with such men directing them in battle; they liked their stump-trained eloquence and their picturesque profanity.

It was inevitable that two such men as Logan and Howard should clash soon or late. As a follower of the preacher-baiting Stephen A. Douglas back in the "Dimocracy" of Illinois, Logan was not one to overvalue religion on the battlefield. The two men were as far apart as the poles, with only one thing in common—a courageous desire for victory.

III

Drama came into the lives of the rival generals shortly before Sherman's armies took Atlanta, and it came also to Howard's fellow-religionists in the West Point tradition—to McPherson and to Leonidas Polk, that firstborn of the Academy's converts.

The Fighting Bishop, as Polk was now called, was a lieutenant general of the Confederacy, tall, fat, monstrously dignified, yet a durable fighter at sixty years of age. He had left the bishopric of Louisiana and his 700 slaves to enter the war with "the cross in one hand and the sword in the other." He was strong and steady if unbrilliant in action, and seemed often on the brink of shouting that favorite command of his brother-general, Cheatham. "Give 'em hell, boys!" But always he checked himself in time to say, "Give 'em—give 'em—er—give 'em what General Cheatham says to give 'em!" Throughout the Confederate Army nobody jeered because he held divine services in camp and field between battles. The Confederate rank and file were more respectful of men in high places than the Westerners of the Union force. Also, constant defeat and weariness made them more ready for spiritual consolation in the summer of 1864.

In Johnston's army the minds of men turned more and more toward Bishop Polk as they fell back in 100 days of incessant fighting toward Atlanta. John B. Hood, the second in command, got religion after the defeat at Resaca. Back in West Point, Hood had not joined Howard, Sooy Smith, and McPherson in professing Christ, but now he was ready. One midnight the bishop, with General Johnston, came by appointment to Hood's tent. A solitary candle furnished the light. Hood, six feet tall, blond-whiskered, his blue eyes always sad as a hound-dog's, rose on his crutches. He had lost a leg at Chickamauga. He tried to kneel when they brought water in a tin basin for the baptism. But he had trouble fumbling at his crutch with his stub of a forearm, for he had lost a hand and wrist at Gettysburg. Seeing his difficulty, the old bishop told him he could sit. But Hood stood, and bowed his head as he was signed to the Lord.

Another day of fighting passed and Polk received a letter from Mrs. Joseph E. Johnston saying that her husband had never been baptized and that she knew the bishop was never too occupied to perform a good deed. She had written Johnston and he awaited Polk's leisure. The next day, May 18, Polk came to Johnston's tent with Hood and Hardee, all Episcopalians now, and baptized their kneeling chief. At the time, men said that Polk looked like George Washington—if one could visualize George Washington in a full white beard.

The desperate campaign went on.

Sometime on June 14, Sherman, reconnoitering the Confederate lines, came to Pine Top, where Howard was peering through his glasses. Six hundred yards away Sherman noticed a group of Confederate officers staring at him.

"How saucy they are!" he snapped. "Howard, make 'em take cover. Have one of your batteries fire three volleys into 'em."

The saucy Confederates were Generals Johnston, Hardee, and Polk, and at the first volley Johnston and Hardee scampered for cover. The fat bishop made off more slowly. Union men, looking on, said that he was too dignified to run. At any rate, he stopped in the open to have another look at the enemy, and a second blast put a shell through him. Johnston and Hardee came back through the cannon balls, put their hands on his forehead, and wept. That evening Union Signal Corps men, reading the Confederates' wigwags, told Sherman that his orders had killed Polk.

Falling back into Atlanta, Johnston was soon removed by the Confederate government for his incessant retreats, and the command was given to Hood, with secret orders to attack. Hearing the news, Sherman called to his headquarters all Yankee officers who might tell him what kind of man Hood was. The West Pointers who had been in class with him said he was rash and impetuous. A Kentucky colonel drawled, "Wall, I seed John Hood onc't bet $2,500 with nary a pa'r in his hand." That settled it. Hood's gambling days might be over, but his nature was still the same. Sherman prepared to withstand an assault.

On July 22 Sherman and McPherson were talking in a farmhouse when a burst of cannon fire rumbling across the woods told them that something was up on the line held by McPherson's divisions. McPherson leaped on his horse and rode toward the roar, scattering his aides with orders as he galloped. In a few minutes only two men were with him, Captain Raymond and Orderly A. C. Thompson.

It was Thompson who, years after, wrote a letter to Sherman, telling what happened on the ride:

The general sent Captain Raymond back with an order; then, when Raymond had got about fifty yards away, General Mc-Pherson turned and started after him, and as near as I can remember, we had got about 150 yards in the woods when I saw Captain Raymond's horse fall. It looked to me like Raymond's horse jumped up about four feet, lit on its back, and slid about a rod. Raymond fell off to the left.

Just as I saw the rebels upon us, they yelled out, "Halt, you damned sons of bitches!" The general checked his horse and raised his hat as if to salute them, and then, with a quick turn to the right, he tried to get away. I saw them raise their guns to shoot. I slid down on my saddle and as I bent over I saw the leaves fly from under the general's horse. My head struck a tree and it stunned me, I suppose, for about three minutes. When I got out of my stun I got up and started to help the general up; he was lying on his right leg with his right hand under his breast; his left hand was on his left leg, and I called him, asking if he was hurt, and he said, "Oh, orderly, I am."

Then I went to pick him up and there was a big rebel caught hold of my revolver belt, and jerked and dragged me away from him, and told me to go to the rear or they would shoot me. At this the general turned over on his face trembling—I think he was dead.

McPherson was dead, right enough, among the leaves. A little later his body was carried to Sherman's head-quarters, where the chief laid it out on chairs and walked up and down beside it, looking at his friend's white face as he barked orders all that day, while the tears ran down his red beard and off on to the floor.

I V

Back on the firing line, the Army of the Tennessee had been bent almost double by the fury of Hood's onslaught, and with no McPherson to rally supports, it might have given way entirely had it not been for the completeness with which John A. Logan filled his dead superior's shoes.

"Black Jack," as the voters of Illinois and the soldiers of the Army called him, was cut out for just such a situation. Hat off, sword in hand, black hair flowing, black walrus mustachios streaming, black eyes blazing—they were so black that the pupils were undefined—his stump-trained voice bellowing "McPherson and revenge," he made the moment so thrillingly theatrical that the Western farmers did the impossible. Outnumbered though they were, they laid down so rapid and deadly a rifle-fire that the Confederates were stopped in writhing heaps. Reinforcements arrived and the Army of the Tennessee, still bellowing something about McPherson, hustled Hood's men back to their trenches.

There was fighting after that, but the Confederacy was done. Bishop Polk was dead; Joe Johnston was sulking at home. Hood had failed and, in a rage, quarreled with both Johnston and Hardee, who had attended him at his baptism so shortly before. Atlanta fell. Hood took his beaten army to Tennessee and smashed it to pieces on the Union breastworks. After the war, he retired to New Orleans, married, and preserved his reputation for impetuosity by becoming the father of two sets of twins.

Sherman, resting his victorious farmers in Atlanta, prepared to reward Logan for his heroism. He planned to promote him to McPherson's place, the position Logan longed for, at the head of the Army of the Tennessee. But General Thomas, commander of another Union wing, the Army of the Cumberland, protested. Since their class-mate days at West Point he had been Old Tom to Sher-man, and Sherman now listened to him. Old Tom was a West Pointer through and through, stolid, formal, punc-tilious, orthodox—a Gibraltar in defensive warfare—the Rock of Chickamauga everybody called him—but slow and unfertile of imagination in attack.

An ancient dislike and distrust of Logan's noisy methods burned inside him. He told Sherman he wouldn't serve alongside the man. Sherman tried to make him forget their old quarrel and finally persuaded him to stick, even with Logan promoted. But in the end, Sherman let Thomas sway him, and for the sake of unity in the Army gave the coveted post to the one man whose elevation would cut Logan most—the "Christian Soldier," Howard.

Logan swallowed his pride and went ahead in his old subordinate position, serving under Howard to the end of the war, but every day he stored up the wrath which he would later pour on the heads of all West Pointers. They had cliqued together against him, he thought.

In after years, Sherman revealed that there had been other factors in his decision. There was the matter of Logan's occasional absence from the Army on stumping-tours back home. Logan answered that he was only obey-ing the private request of Lincoln. Eventually the two veterans patched up their quarrel, but not before Logan, as Congressman and Senator from Illinois and chairman of the committee on military appropriations, had given

Sherman, the Regular Army, and West Point some harrowing hours.

Logan led the fight that slashed Sherman's peacetime salary and reduced the number of officers. Worse, he spoke and wrote most persuasively against West Point regulars who drew fat pay while G.A.R. veterans with peg-legs and empty sleeves starved on pitifully small pensions. He published a book, *The American Volunteer Soldier*, which glorified the men who had entered the service from civil life and which castigated West Point for its snobbery, caste follies, and military ineptitude. Sold on subscription through the G.A.R., whose commander Logan now was, this book was widely read. In Congress there was talk, now and then, of abolishing the Academy altogether. A prolonged reaction against the Regular Army set in, and much of the sentiment which was to keep it low in numbers arose from Logan's fiery oratory.

And while the agitation was afoot there was nothing that a volunteer veteran could say with more damning effect than "West Point's a great place to make preachers."

Billy the Kid

The statement of Tom Blevins (see pages 3 and 67) given to me in his cabin near Jensen, Utah, on the night of November 1, 1930.

THIS Billy the Kid was twenty-two years and twenty-two days when he died. He told me he was born in Albany, New York, and he said his name was William Borney. I forget what big college he said he went to back East before he come West, but he landed in New Mexico in 1876 and went to work for the Blank Cattle company. He was between seventeen and eighteen then, a small fellow and as pleasant a man as you'd ever want for to see. He worked there for them rich men for about two years and in that time he got to stealin' a lot of cattle and he was so smart nobody could find out who was doin' it.

Now, here I've got to talk about a fellow I don't want to name. Some of his folks may be livin' and shy about havin' it told on him, so I'll call him Charley—Old Charley.

Well, Old Charley had a big outfit and, of all the cow rows in the West, him and the Blanks had the biggest. Old Charley kept losin' cattle and blamin' it on the Blanks, but the stuff he was losin' was what Billy had took. The stealin' was gettin' worse every summer, so Old Charley got to lookin' around and seen that Billy was a reckless sort of fellow and a leader, so he come to him and he said,

"Billy, I'll give you $10,000 a year if you'll deliver me 10,000 of them Blank cattle and besides I'll give you $200 a month to ride my herds."

Billy went to work for him and in two months he'd delivered the cattle. Then Old Charley was so anxious to run the Blanks out that he told Billy he'd give him a thousand dollars for every Blank cowboy he killed, but nobody knowed about any of this 'til later.

Well, this time I'm a-goin' to tell you about there was eight cow outfits of us camped at Roselle. Roselle was ten miles west of Cottonwood Crossin' on the Pagos and had an outfittin' store and Old George Gail's saloon. Billy was around there awhile, but he'd been gone ten days when we moved down to the Crossin'.

The second morning after we got there, there come a big heavy flood-like down the Pagos and a fellow seen a body in it. We hauled it out and then they come floatin' down so fast we just stood on the bank and watched for 'em to drag 'em out. We drug out eleven men, most of 'em shot between the eyes. We buried 'em and went on about our work. And the first thing, by God, in come Billy the Kid. He was well educated and could make a splendid talk, and after supper he said to me, "Tom, I've got ten horses, and I want to ride with the wagon down the Pagos and pick up." He says, "I'll ride with you. You're nearer my age than some of these cranky old devils."

Then's when I opened a hornets' nest, for I says, "All right, Billy, but everything's to be on the square." I liked Billy, but I'd heard rumors about him stealin' Blank cattle for Old Charley, though I didn't know nothin' about him killin' men.

Billy says, "Old Charley owes me $20,000 and, God damn him, he's got to pay me. I'm goin' to cut out my horses right now and get my pay."

So he did. Old Charley was at the ranch when he rode up.

"God damn you, Charley, I've come after my pay," he says.

Old Charley says, "What you've done you'll get pay for. I'll check up on you."

Billy says, "I've put ten of the Blank riders out, and I don't want to give it away."

Old Charley says, "Well, you won't get paid for it 'til I get better word than yours."

Billy says, "I've done my work. The Blanks owe me one-third as much as you. I'm goin' to collect that, too."

"I don't know about this workin' for two outfits," Charley says.

Billy says, "Between you, you owe me a lot of money and I ain't ever goin' to work for wages again. I've got money and I've got money comin' and I'm goin' to get it."

So he rode off over to White Oaks, a cow town about eighty miles off, to see Pat Garrett, a deputy U. S. marshal who was sick there, and Billy says, "Pat, I've been gettin' dirt from two outfits and I want to tell you I'm goin' to collect. Now we've been friends"—Billy had paid Pat's bills in the hospital where he was layin' awhile before this—"and I don't want to hurt you, but they'll be after you to get me and I want to warn you not to come. Now I've bought you some clothes and here's $200 'til you get well. Now, Pat, remember I told you. Things is goin' to break out here in pretty good shape." And he went away.

Old Charley went to Chicago about that time to see the Morris Packin' Company about the money he had comin' from 17,000 steers he'd sent 'em, and Billy was someway onto this and found out when Old Charley was comin' back, so he rode to a spring on the trail about halfway between Old George Gail's saloon and Los Vegas where Old Charley would have to come along.

Well, Old Charley come back and put the money in the Los Vegas bank and rode on down toward home all dressed up like a boy again. He'd got him some new Chicago clothes and had him a new saddle and, as he come prancin' along, Billy stepped out and threw down on him.

"Charley, I'm glad to meet you," he says.

Charley says, "Yes, Billy, I'm glad to meet you."

"Are you ready to settle that bill?"

And Charley says, "I don't know yet that you've earned it."

"God damn you, I'll pay myself," and he shot Old Charley's horse and stuck his gun in Charley's face and said, "I won't kill you. I'll just torture you."

Old Charley had his hands helt up and Billy tied 'em together, and he says, "Come over here, Charley. I've got a nice comfortable place in the shade, and I want you to write a check. I want you to live for about ten years to enjoy all this rottenness you've done me."

Charley had only $10,000 in the bank, he said, and he'd write Billy a check for that and give him the rest later. He said it was all right, and Billy says, "All right? I know it's all right and I know you're good because I'm goin' to make you good."

So Billy untied Old Charley's hands, took the check, and then tied Old Charley to a cedar better and rode all night, and in the mornin' he got the money when the bank opened and got a gallon of whiskey and brought it back to Old Charley.

"I want to see you drink this," he says. "Open your mouth. I'm goin' to make you drink half of this now and the other half for supper."

Old Charley says, "Billy, we've been pretty good friends—"

But Billy he says, "Yes, you've got rich too fast to not be a misery to the people."

Well, sundown comes and Billy says, "Look here. I'd look better in them clothes—them Chicago clothes." And he undressed Old Charley, and he couldn't make head nor tail of a union suit Old Charley had got him in Chicago, and it was the first, too, that had ever been brought into that country, but he experimented 'til he got it on and then when Old Charley was stark naked, Billy poured a lot more whiskey down him and started him walkin' barefoot for home. Old Charley had his nerve so high after all that liquor and excitement that he went steppin' off fast through the moonlight and Billy went back to the spring and went to sleep.

Old Charley got in about dead.

Well, the way things happen, nine of Charley's punchers, out lookin' for Charley, come into the spring about sunup. Billy got their attention on the clothes business, and then shot eight of 'em like a flash, and he says to the last one, "I want you to take the news back that Billy the Kid will kill every man ridin' one of Old Charley's horses."

The fellow went back and found Old Charley and told him.

Just then the Blanks, lookin' fer their men, found where they was buried down by Cottonwood Crossin' and who done it, so both outfits threw in together and got Pat Garrett to run Billy down.

Pat organized ten men, and while he was organizin', Billy heard about it and went up to White Oaks and seen Pat and told him, "Now I can kill you any time, but I don't want to. I've only done what I ought to, and if everybody'd do that, this here would be a heap better country."

Billy went off and organized, too, and took some men who was glad to follow him and went over to the Walker Ranch, a little outfit at the foot of the Capitan Mountains at the head of a little-bitty creek called Peeance. Walker was from the East and had his wife in a real nice place with three or four rooms and had a piano, and Billy landed there with three men. Walker, he didn't know Billy, but seein' what a nice fellow he was and smart, he hired him to watch the ranch while he went back to Illinois to let his wife visit her folks.

One night Pat Garrett and his gang surrounded the house and went up close to talk. "Kid," he says, "we're after you and the best thing is surrender."

Billy calls out, "Look here, Pat! I've told you to stay away. Now go back and if you come within sixty-five yards I'll kill you."

It come along dark and Pat and his gang crawled up. Billy saw 'em, and a fellow named Baker crawled up the closest and Billy shot him. Old Pat he up the white flag and called, "I'm for havin' a council."

Billy yelled, "One more step and I'll kill you. Go back.

I'm goin' to stay here as long as I want and when I'm ready I'm goin' on."

Pat camped within 600 yards and next morning here he was with a white flag again. "We can't have any argument," he yelled. "I'll send in two men halfway to that cottonwood to talk. I've been sent to get you and I'm goin' to do it."

The Kid come out with a man and they met them others at the cottonwood and Billy said, "The move is up to you. Promise to go home and I'll not kill you. We'll kill all sixteen of you or be killed."

They quit and all started back, and Pat's two men had got about 150 yards when the man with Billy pulled his gun and shot one of them in the back and then Billy killed the other one and then Pat's men, the whole God damned cheese, lammed away and Billy made it back, but the fellow with him was killed. Then the shootin' commenced. Billy had killed seven by night, so Pat said, "We'll quit her 'til morning."

He'd sent word back to the fort and the next morning up come 300 nigger soldiers, and they surrounded the house and their captain come up with a white flag and Billy yelled to him to go back and he didn't and Billy killed him. The soldiers counciled and counciled and there was 300 of 'em, and this sergeant who'd took command, he says for 'em to oil the house good as soon as night come and set her afire. Billy and his partner shot five niggers, but they kept comin' and got her afire. Billy shot some more but it was no use he seen—they were to take him—so when the soldiers fell back 100 yards to wait, he stayed in just as long as he could.

The house was burnin' like a house afire by this time

and Billy went to the piano—he could play the best you ever heard—and he sung "Home, Sweet Home" as pretty as you please, and then got up and threw open the door and hollered, "Watch them niggers jump," and come out shootin' with both hands and broke through, but his man behind him was killed. He shot twelve niggers gettin' through and him and his band had killed thirty-five men in the fight.

He run to the soldiers' camp and picked out the best horse and pulled for the plains of Texas.

Well, the nigger soldiers, they went back to Fort Sumner, but Pat Garrett and six men kept followin' Billy about two days behind. By the time Billy had got to Big Salt Lake in Texas some other guy had dropped in with him and they come to a rock dugout near Newman's DZ-brand outfit. Pat and his men come up and found 'em in there and, just like always, Billy hollered out, "I don't want to kill you," but Pat didn't pay no attention to that. So Billy and the fellow got their canteens full of water and opened the door and rode out shootin', and he killed three men and enough horses to put Garrett's outfit on foot, but the man that had been with him was caught. Then Billy disappeared fer awhile and all anybody knowed was Pat was still on his trail.

I was around Old George Gail's saloon about this time; it was right on our range and after awhile Billy come there in disguise. He had whiskers and had changed his manners, but we all knowed him and said nothin'. He'd come back to get another $10,000 from Old Charley. He went right to Old Charley, and Old Charley said, "Now, Billy, you leave, and I'll pay you still more. You sign a contract and I'll pay you. Either leave here or else leave people alone."

Billy says, "No, when I get ready to leave I'll leave. I'm goin' to have some fun with the $10,000 amongst my friends—the boys that's tryin' to earn their money," and he rode off.

Well, Old Charley had lost $50,000 because nobody would want to hire to him, Billy havin' killed so many of his men by that time, and then besides, whenever Billy would catch Old Charley out by himself, he'd strip him and I reckon he must have sent Old Charley home afoot naked five times in a year. So Old Charley paid him and went to Chicago to stay 'til Billy was dead or had left.

Billy come into Roselle with the money and loafed around Old George Gail's saloon. Cowboys was comin' in and gettin' on busts. Billy had got meaner, but he took a notion to break out in good shape, and the first few days he spent money on the boys and felt kind.

Then there was a man named Charley Van Zandt who come in with a tent. He knowed there'd be lots of outfits there to rest up for two weeks, and he had all sorts of goods in a tent a hundred feet long with a big counter down through the middle of it and an immense quantity of second-handed suits and shirts and such like.

Old George Gail had added on a big gamblin' hall to his saloon and had put in eight or ten tables that he'd rent to these God damned tin-horns—these gamblers from Los Vegas—and he'd furnish each table with $250 and take ten per cent of what they made.

This night I'm tellin' you about there was maybe a hundred of us cowboys layin' around and in come Billy. Old George was a whole-hearted sort of a fellow and a good friend of Billy's, and so he set 'em up when Billy come in about ten o'clock. Billy says, "By God, we're goin' to have some fun this trip, we're goin' to have some real fun. I've got $10,000, and none of you boys owns any stock in this company I'm runnin'. I'm goin' to be like Jay Gould for once. Have you got a bed, Tom? for I'm comin' to sleep with you when it's over."

By midnight everybody was drunk, and I says, "Billy, I'm goin' to the wagons. Things is goin' to be on the trail early in the morning."

"Wait, Tom," he says. "We ain't been to this gamblin' hall yet."

"All right," I says, "I may win a fortune yet."

"If you don't I'll take it away from these God damned tin-horns."

"Don't injure Old George," I says. "He's got an interest in them tables."

"No," he says, "a man that would injure Old George would go to hell sure."

Him and I was drinkin' with John Pledger and Billy says, "There's a man in there with more money than he needs and he's not of our race, anyway." So we started for the gamblin' hall and I was pretty good at faro so I went over in the back to play that, and I'd been there about an hour when I heard a shot and seen Billy draggin' a Mexican monte dealer, California Mike—a galvanized Mexican—away by the heels and holding his face on the money all the time and he says, "Now, boys, keep away from that money. It's Old George's. I'll run this game from now on and, by God, I'm goin' to make Old George some money."

Billy had put a hundred dollars down and California

Mike had taken it, and Billy had put down another hundred dollars and California Mike had taken that, too, and Billy says, "By God, don't look like you cowboys would git much tonight," and he put down another hundred and lost that and so he just reached out and raked the money all in. California Mike reached for his gun, but it caught on the table and Billy shot him.

"We'll just bury him in the morning," he says. "Business is too rushin' now," and California Mike laid out there like a steer and Billy got to dealin' and lost, so in about two or three hours, he says, "We'll quit," and he took the money and threw in a lot more just for Old George, and we all went off to other tables and got to gamblin' to beat the band.

Then Van Zandt lit the lights in his tent, for morning was comin' and all the God damn cheese got to drinkin' harder than ever.

Billy looked out and seen daylight comin' over those long 100-mile flats and he says, "Now every man in this outfit come with me. I've had this peddler come here to see you God damn cowboys was dressed right for once." And in a minute that circus tent was full of men tryin' on corduroy suits and hats and shirts, and Van Zandt was busy tickled with business, and Billy brought in his horse and tied its tail to the end of a roll of white sheetin', and Van Zandt come up and wanted his money for the stuff the cowboys was buyin' and Billy says, "You'd better tend to this funeral we're goin' to have first."

The peddler says, "I ain't goin' to furnish for no funeral."

And Billy says, "You're just bein' introduced to the furnishin' business," and he jumped on his horse and out he went and there was white sheetin' all over the county and the peddler runnin' around in a faint.

Billy rode the roll out, then we went into the saloon and give Old George $10,000 and told him to let the boys drink what they wanted and take out everything and hold the rest for him.

Well, eleven o'clock come, the time somebody'd set for the funeral and there was no grave dug. The cowboys was all too drunk and Billy says, "You boys is too well dressed to dig a grave. We'll just make the peddler dig the grave."

He rode into the tent and says to Van Zandt, "How are you feelin'?"

Van Zandt says, "Good."

Billy says, "We want a grave dug."

Van Zandt says, "Ain't they plenty of cowboys?"

"Yes," says Billy, "but they're too well dressed and they ain't used to it. Now you dig that grave in thirty minutes or I'll kill you. Get your three brothers or whatever they are there to help you or I'll dig four graves and, by God, I'll fill 'em."

So the peddler he hurried and the four brothers they dug it pretty good and we all gathered up the sheetin' and drug the dead gambler up there to the grave and Billy says, "Now you peddlers roll him up," and the Van Zandts rolled California Mike up and had a counsultation with themselves, and some cowboy said, "Goin' to bury this man like a dog?"

"No," says Billy, "these peddlers will preach."

But they wouldn't, and one cowboy said a few remarks about what a son-of-a-bitch California Mike was and Billy says, "Now you peddlers let him down while we pray," and we all took off our hats and Van Zandt says, "This man's dead and should have decent burial."

And Billy says, "You Christ-killin' sons-a-bitches, how much decenter burial do you expect to see a man git than this man's a-gettin'? We're showin' him every respect; our financial standing will let us."

Van Zandt says, "Looky here. We'll cover him up, but we won't have anything to do with this prayin' racket and we want pay for this sheetin'."

Well, just then Old George—he was a sympathizin' kind of a fellow—come up and got 'em to finish off a nice burial and we went back to the tent—Old George could lead any bunch—and we held a general jubilee with cow-boys squallin' and ridin' all over the county, and the peddler come up with a bill for $3,000 and Old George paid him $1,500. So when Billy and all of us had got sobered down next day, George had took out all expenses all round and the cowboys had had a pretty good benefit. Billy said it was all right and took the money that was left and lit out for Lincoln County, New Mexico, to see the town of Lincoln. He was about a month or two gettin' there and Pat Garrett had beat him in and had left a de-scription with Fountain Campbell, the sheriff. Billy took his horse to the wagon-yard, and come on into the saloon and took four or five drinks and then went up to the hotel, and Fountain Campbell come in unknown to Billy and set alongside him eatin' and talkin' and got Billy to laughin', and a deputy closed in behind and they grabbed Billy and handcuffed him. They read a warrant and Campbell said, "Now, finish yer meal with one hand, fer I'll have to lock you up till you're recognized. Garrett will be here in a few days," and Billy laughed and eat his supper out and they set around fer awhile. The sheriff and his deputy liked Billy. He was an awful good entertainer.

Four days later Pat got in with three deputies and swore out the warrants proper and right and sent fer a judge and they helt the trial and sentenced Billy to be hung in six days.

Billy and two deputies went up to the hotel to get their meals. Pat Garrett said he'd stay and watch Billy, and Fountain Campbell went off about his business.

Well, the day before Billy was to be hung at four-twenty in the afternoon, Pat says to the deputies, "To-morrow is to be Billy's last day and he's got to be watched awful close till we hang him. I've got to go away tonight, but I'll be back here fer the hangin'."

Billy laughed and says, "I'll be there."

That next day they'd gathered about thirty of us cow-boys in to see how the thing went.

Well, there was a blacksmith right by the jail and he kept a good horse. At breakfast time one deputy went after the breakfast and left Billy handcuffed to the other deputy. He throwed Billy a newspaper. Billy was a great reader. Somebody must have given Billy a sign, fer when the deputy bringin' the breakfast was about sixty yards away, Billy shot from underneath the newspaper and got the deputy beside him under the right jaw and then he run to the door and drawed down on the other deputy and made him kneel.

"Let's see you pray," he said and, as the deputy kneeled down, Billy emptied five shots into him and then pulled the dead man that was handcuffed to him into the black-smith shop and laid his hand on the anvil and said, "Cut me loose or out comes yer brains."

We'd heerd the shootin' and run up in time to see the blacksmith cuttin' away cool as ice.

I never knowed but I always thought he was in on it. Another thing, the blacksmith's boy come runnin' up and Billy says, "Go, bring your horse!" And he says to the blacksmith, "How much fer your horse?"

"I don't think I want to sell him," says the blacksmith.

"All right," says Billy, "I'll leave him at such and such a place." I couldn't make out where it was he said it was.

Billy got on the horse and rode up the hill where the courthouse was and all them judges and lawyers that had decided to hang him, they was nowhere to be seen. There was just him on his horse and the rest of us lookin' at him up the little raise. He was just as happy as he waved his hat—he had a big Mexican hat—and he yelled, "Good-bye, boys. Next time I see you I guess it'll be in hell," and he rode off and I never seen him again.

I never could figure out how he got that gun. Maybe Pat Garrett was in on it. It was sure funny how he got it.

We'd have never see him hung. That's why we had gathered in there. Why, some of us was still wearin' the corduroys he'd bought us out of Van Zandt's tent. We was just waitin' till the day of the hangin' so's we could gather in Garrett while we was rescuin' Billy.

Billy was as well-mannered a fellow as you'd ever see. Well educated in books and music. Cowpunchers liked his manners, and he was never stuck up in this world.

He was always on cobweb standin'—liable to drop through to hell any minute.

Well, along about this time, Billy says to a friend, "They'll kill me. I want to see Annie Maxwell before I die."

Billy had loved Annie Maxwell for years. He had got to know her back in Ottaway, Illinois, where his sisters lived. There was two of his sisters back there and he'd met up with Annie visitin' them. Annie was a fine-lookin' girl away up in society back there in Ottaway, Illinois, and she would come down every summer to visit her old bachelor brother, Pete Maxwell, who had bought Fort Sumner from the government.

Billy the Kid never mixed up with whores.

He was just as pleasant as though nothin' was botherin' him in the world. He could go to bed and sleep as sound as anybody but he was awful easy waked. I fergit what college he said he'd left when he come West.

Well, Pat Garrett had kept watchin' the Maxwell outfit, waitin' fer Billy to come to see Annie. Pete Maxwell didn't know Garrett, and so Pat and three of his deputies went there and stayed and boarded. Old Pete was rich.

Three nights after they got there the moon filled.

Billy come ridin' up to the cook shack and said to the old Mexican cook, "Jesus Christ, my feet hurt and I'm hungry."

The cook says, "I'll go wake Pete up while this coffee boils and git the key to the storeroom to git you some meat."

Billy says, "No, I'll get the key," and he took his boots in his hand and started out. He come to the great big porch and there was three deputies hidin' in the bushes and they seen Billy walk along in the shadow of the porch roof close to the house with a gun in his hand past the big windows.

The moon was shinin' fine and the deputies hid more so. Billy thought it was goats and went on to the door and knocked. Pat Garrett was sleepin' with Old Pete Maxwell in what had used to be the officers' room and Pat was next to the wall. Old Pete calls out, "Who's that?" and Billy only knocked again. Pete said, "There's Billy," and Billy walked in shy and easy.

"That you, Pete?" he says.

"Yes, this is me, Billy," Pete says.

"I've come for the key to the storeroom," and he walked into the moonlight from one of them big windows, and as he did that, Pat shot over Old Pete and got Billy through the heart. And as he went down he called out, "Who's that in with you, Pete?" and he shot over Pete and the bullet cut through Pete's shirt into the wall, and Billy went down, but he shot five more times into the floor before he died.

Pat Garrett was so scared he shot his next shot into the ceilin' and him and Old Pete laid there sweatin'!

After a bit, Pete says, "I guess you've killed him."

"Yes," says Pat, "I've killed a good friend—if he's really dead. He may come alive again. Call to them deputies to come and look in the window and see!"

Pete called and the deputies peeked in the window and seen Billy layin' with his head in a pool of moonshine. They wouldn't come in until about an hour and wouldn't then, I reckon, if the Mexican cook hadn't come up to see what was the trouble about the meat. He walked right in and says, "Has Billy got the key?"

"No," Pete says, "I guess he's dead there."

The old Mexican says, "He's cold. You've killed the best friend I ever had."

So then they got up.

Annie was back in Illinois on a visit and they tilly-graphed her and his sisters and, in about two months, they come and took his body back to Ottaway.

But as Pat and Pete and the deputies was layin' him out, Pete says, "Pat, you'll have bad luck. Your life ain't worth much." They buried Billy in the soldiers' buryin' ground the next day. All that interested Pat was the reward, $12,000 from the state and $32,000 from the cow association. Well, he got the reward and went to ranchin' near Elephant Butte Dam on the Rio Grande. He run a bunch of goats and hired a boy to herd 'em. He come along in a buggy one mornin' pretty early and seen the goats out on the road and after a while the boy come up. He'd been shootin' geese and Pat started to whip him and the boy blowed Pat's head off.

They claim it hurt Annie Maxwell bad when she heard Billy was dead. She never married, and when she went back with the body, she never come into that country again. A few years afterwards Pete sold out and went back to civilization.

Annie was twenty-two years old, the same as Billy when he was killed. She knowed he was a killer, but I guess that only made her stuck on him all the more so.

Billy, whenever he'd see any of us on the range, he'd ask if we seen anything of Annie or if she'd sent any mail.

Well, he'd run things in pretty good shape; he'd put the Blanks out of business and pretty near Old Charley, too, and he'd collected, I guess, anyways $50,000 off them two outfits and spent it on his friends, and he'd killed lots of gamblers that was robbin' the cowpunchers, and he'd sent lots of money back to his folks and presents to Annie.

He was never a talkative man. He'd laugh and be

pleasant and could get people to like him fine without havin' to say much to do it.

Often he'd say to me while pullin' off his boots around the wagon, after I'd been handlin' the boys in a big stampede or drive, "Tom, if I could control myself like you, I'd be in no trouble and have a big stake, too."

I'd tell him that I didn't care for money any more than for potatoes and he'd say, "I ain't that way. Whenever I see a man with a lot of money, I want to distribute it among the boys."

And that gambler he killed in Old George Gail's saloon I was tellin' you about, his name was California Frank—I said California Mike—that was wrong. It was California Frank, that's what it was.

The Rats and Cats
at Terre Haute

CHICAGO'S leading volunteer authority on matters theatrical is George Wharton, one-time leader of the loop-hound pack, and of summer afternoons he lets his memory have full sway.

"Vaudeville is terrible now," he said yesterday. "No animal acts. I like animals; they're very interesting. When I was managing vaudeville theaters, I'd spend hours backstage talking to the trainers and feeding the animals.

"There was one act I'll never forget—the best I ever saw—a lot of rats and cats all together. I saw it for the first time at Springfield, Illinois, where it came to my theater. Very funny. Just a lot of alley cats and rats riding on each other's backs, walking tight ropes and holding hands.

"After the first show, there I was backstage asking questions about the act. The trainer said he kept them happy by keeping 'em full of food. They were always so full up they couldn't eat each other.

"'Well,' I said, 'your act's great, great. All it lacks is a big smash finish.'

"He said he knew it. He said he had had a big smash finish, but the Orpheum officials wouldn't let him use it on account of an accident that had happened in Terre Haute three weeks earlier.

"The fellow said it was just his luck to have the accident happen when a traveling official of the circuit was in the house and could ban the whole finish.

" 'It was a wonderful finale,' he said with tears in his eyes. 'I put lace caps on all the cats and rats and loaded 'em in a baby buggy and wheeled 'em slowly across the stage. That was all. That was enough. It panicked the crowds. The sight of all them cats and rats in each other's laps was sweet.

" 'Well, sir,' he said, 'I was wheeling 'em across the stage at Terre Haute and the house was wild with applause, wild, I tell you. Some women were in tears. But it was just my luck to have a wheel come off the baby buggy in the middle of the big promenade—and it had to be a wheel next the audience. Before you could bat your eye those cats and rats were all out of their nightdresses and baby caps and had poured over the footlights like a washtub full of water.

" 'Such shrieking I never heard. The people broke for the doors. The aisles were full of women trampling big strong men underfoot, and a lot of women—good, plump, small-town matrons—didn't bother about the aisles. They just h'isted up their skirts and started jumping seats, one row after another, till they got to the back of the house. It looked like hurdlers at a track meet, and every time they'd jump they'd yell.'

" 'That was the awful part of it. They scared my rats and cats almost to death with their screaming.

" 'The house was clear inside of three minutes. Those people used every exit, and some of 'em made new exits in the walls. I had the house manager turn up the lights, and I stood out in the middle of the auditorium callin' for my cats and rats to come back. I tossed cheese around on the floor and I whistled and sung and talked nice to 'em. After awhile I saw a pair of bright eyes coming 'round the end of a row of seats and a rat ran down and up my pants leg and sat on my shoulder trembling. Pretty soon a cat looked down over the balcony rail, saw me, and jumped to a box and then onto the stage and the floor and crawled up on my shoulder and snuggled down beside the rat for company.

" 'It took me three hours to get 'em all back, but I did it. No, not all of 'em. One rat didn't show up for two days. He came sneaking out of the wings during a show, forty-eight hours after the calamity—just sneaked out and crawled up on the little tight rope and began doing his stuff without a word. I guess he'd been on a drunk.' "

A Hymn from an Abattoir

MOST men who have written hymns have come, soon or late, to believe the Lord God Jehovah to be the real author of their compositions, and themselves to be little more than inspired stenographers. They have felt, no doubt sincerely, that this attitude was the ultimate in modesty, and it may be piously wondered if any of them ever recognized what conceit they proclaimed.

Philip Paul Bliss, however, was a truly humble man. Not only did he give the Almighty full credit for his amazing output of hymns; he also gave Him nearly all his royalties. The popularity which floated him on its tide from 1870 to 1876 never appeared to touch his vanity. It was a Higher Power, not he, who had written those gospel songs which practically every pious American Protestant seemed to be singing, and that Higher Power, he thought, should get back the proceeds in the form of contributions to evangelism.

So irresistible were Bliss's revival songs that scores of them continued as favorites as late as 1900, and some of them are employed even today by bucolic revivalists. What Sunday-school scholar of the elder generation has never sung "Hold the Fort," "Pull for the Shore," "What Shall the Harvest Be?", "Only an Armor-bearer," "Almost Persuaded," "Oh! That Will Be Heaven for Me," "Let the Lower Lights Be Burning," "Jesus Loves Even Me," and the rest of the Bliss masterpieces?

Bliss's singing and exhorting were celebrated through the midlands and South in the middle 'Seventies. His baritone voice was thrilling and his handsome face beamed with kindness behind his big, black beard. What delight he took and gave when, at the end of a hymn, he told his hearers how divine inspiration had made him write it! Particularly was he sure of that inspiration in "Hold the Fort."

"Its use in churches all round the world," he would say, "is on account of its harmony with the word of God upon a truth intended to arouse Christians. Let us sing it— Number eleven!"

Then, with the organ swelling into that warlike melody, men, women and children would begin:

> Ho! my comrades, see the signal
>   Waving in the sky;
> Reinforcements now appearing;
>   Victory is nigh!

> "Hold the fort, for I am coming,"
>   Jesus answers still;
> Wave the answer back to Heaven:
>   "By Thy grace, we will."

Had any of the singers stopped to inquire into the genesis of the song, its words might have stuck in their throats, for the historical incident that inspired it was one of those upon which William Tecumseh Sherman based his decision that war is hell. Bliss took his idea from a Civil War battle which, in its lavish scattering of blood, brains, and viscera, was, in proportion to numbers involved, one of the worst of the whole war. It is a commentary upon the blinding power of religion that none of the Southern-

ers with whom he sang the hymn so often ever observed
that the loathed Sherman was the Jesus of the song, and
that its Satan was none other than their own revered Confederacy, now so tragically lost.

I I

After Sherman captured Atlanta on September 1, 1861,
the Southern strategy was to force him to withdraw to
the North whence he had come. So the one-legged, one-
armed General John B. Hood struck at his communications, falling upon the railroad that stretched northwest
of the city. Unfortunately for Hood, his chief executive,
Jefferson Davis, gave away the campaign secret in a series
of stump-speeches that warned Sherman in time to be
prepared.

Sherman sent to Nashville, at the other end of the
line, enough men to handle Hood when he should arrive,
and put over this army his most dependable officer,
Major General George H. Thomas, the Rock of Chickamauga. That done, he waited until Hood launched his
drive, and then fell upon his rear and harried him toward
Thomas. Once he saw that Hood was on his way, he returned to Atlanta and his leisurely task of disemboweling
Georgia and both Carolinas. Soon afterward news came
that Hood had shattered himself against Thomas at the
Battle of Nashville.

At the start of the campaign, however, Hood had given
Sherman an anxious day or two, by swooping down upon
a major supply depot at Allatoona Pass, sixty miles up the
track from Atlanta. Here on a mountain height protected
by two small forts, one on each side of a deep railroad

cut, were warehouses holding a million rations of Union hardtack. In the rocky valleys five miles away grazed 9,000 cattle destined to become beefsteaks for bluecoats. To man the forts Sherman had left Lieutenant Colonel Tourtelotte and 941 cavalry, a force too small for comfort once thousands of gray infantry began to pour into the region.

On October 4, Sherman, starting after Hood, learned that the Confederate division commander, S. G. French, was nearing Allatoona and that the telegraph wires had been cut. Quickly he had his signalmen wigwag a call for help from one mountain peak to another across the heads of the enemy. The force nearest Allatoona was that of Brigadier General John Murray Corse at Rome, Georgia, forty miles from the Pass on a branch railroad. Corse, fortunately, was the man for just such an emergency.

Immediately after his graduation from West Point in 1857, he had resigned from the army to practice law and politics in Iowa. So precipitate was his personality that he had been nominated and defeated for Lieutenant-Governor on the Democratic ticket, and had left for the war, sore and angry, by the early summer of 1861. As a major of the 6th Iowa Volunteers, he had fought viciously under Grant and Sherman and had won his brigadier-general's stars during the Atlanta campaign.

When Sherman's signal came to him on the evening of October 4, Corse struck off for Allatoona immediately with 1,000 of his men inside and on top of box-cars. So recklessly did he hurry his engineer that the narrow, rickety rails spread behind the train and prevented a second load of his men from following. Unaware of this misfortune, Corse and his 1,000 arrived at Allatoona a little after midnight, to find the garrison under arms and peering at the fires which the Confederates were making out of railroad ties and the little blockhouses down in the valley. Tourtelotte was feverishly trying to teach 200 recruits how to handle their muskets.

Corse took the west fort, Tourtelotte the east and, between them, they divided the six cannon and communicated with each other across a narrow bridge made of two pine trees, spanning the railroad cut.

At the rear of the forts rose the mountain; on each flank, at the base of the ridge, ran creeks walled with pines. For some 200 yards on three sides all the trees had been felled to give the riflemen full play, and midway of this distance Tourtelotte had planted a row of sharpened stakes to impede attackers. But at best the defenders were only so many targets on a bald hill. Their breastworks were low and could be easily enfiladed if assailed by massed artillery on three sides.

This disadvantage was seen at dawn when the Confederate batteries unlimbered. The Union men flattened themselves behind their parapets and endured it. At eight o'clock the bombardment stopped and a gray-clad major was seen climbing the hill and waving a white flag. He bore a message from General French to the commanding officer:

I have placed the forces under my command in such positions that you are surrounded, and to avoid a needless effusion of blood I call upon you to surrender your forces at once, and unconditionally. Five minutes will be allowed you to decide. Should you accede to this, you will be treated in the most honorable manner as prisoners of war.

In the bushes beyond the shaved semicircle surrounding the forts, the Confederate infantrymen watched anxiously. Their haversacks were empty, and their mouths watered for the million Union rations which French had promised that they should have by ten o'clock that morning.

Up on the hill, however, Corse was dooming them to disappointment. Without hesitating a moment, he wrote, on a stump, this answer:

> Your communication demanding surrender of my command I acknowledge receipt of and respectfully reply that we are prepared for the "needless effusion of blood" whenever it is agreeable to you.
>
> I am, respectfully, your obedient servant, etc.

III

Somehow, in the confusion, the answer was never delivered to French, but comprehending, he gave the word; the batteries roared, and thereafter, for three hours and a half, the hill was an abattoir, torn every which way by red explosions which kicked jagged iron into the sides, backs, and faces of men. Corse, cocked pistol in hand and scorning cover, strode up and down behind his riflemen, swearing fiercely at those who showed despair. Nobody ran away: there was no place to run to. Shells and rifle-balls swept in from three sides.

The Union cannoneers toiled in the open as became their trade. Crew after crew were blown away from their guns in the storm of Southern lead. At length the gunners had to lie on their backs and pass ammunition over their heads to the man at the muzzle. He would sit up, ram home the charge, then lie down while a comrade sprang to the breech, aimed the piece, and pulled the lanyard.

While the cannonade raged, Sherman climbed Kenesaw Mountain, fourteen miles away as crows flew across the autumn woods. He was anxious about Allatoona and must see how it fared. About 8 A.M. he came to the little log-shanty on the summit where his signal corps operated with wigwag flags by day and flaming torches by night. From its dark interior a telescope protruded and through this telescope signal officers eyed stations on the peaks for thirty miles around.

The morning of October 5 was a beautiful one, Sherman always remembered, with the red and yellow and green forest flaming at his feet. All that could be seen of Allatoona was a cloud of white smoke. "Find out if Corse is there," Sherman snapped, and a signal man began waving dark flags against the bright background of the sky.

Over in Allatoona's east fort signalmen standing among the shells watched Kenesaw, for it was the center of communication for the whole region. They caught Sherman's question. Tourtelotte said, "Answer that Corse is here with a portion of his brigade and we must have reinforcements." A flagman stood on a stump and began sending. He had spelled out "Corse is here with—" when a shell cut his staff in two.

Sherman's officer at the Kenesaw telescope kept losing letters as the distant flag was alternately hidden and revealed by the billowing smoke. Finally he came out of the shanty saying, "General, I can't make out anything from what I have here—C.S.H.E.H.E." Sherman studied the letters for a moment and then exclaimed: "I understand it—Corse is there all right! He'll hold out. I know the man."

Nevertheless, he said to General Willard Warner, beside him, "General, go down and telegraph General Cox [a division commander close at hand] to move on French's rear, and make French understand he can't stay there with Corse in his front and Cox in his rear. Tell Cox to burn every house and barn that he comes to so that I can see where he is all the time."

Warner sped away and Sherman turned back to the telescope. When noon came, the Confederates around Allatoona slackened their fire. They were going to try their infantry. Corse knew the signs and braced for the shock. Whosoever among the wounded could aim a rifle was brought up to the parapet. Cannons were crammed with canister, loose shot, pecks of Minié balls.

With a yell, the hungry, dirty gray-coats came out of the woods, shooting as they ran. One hundred yards from the entrenchments stood Tourtelotte's row of sharpened stakes. Corse told his men to hold their fire until the enemy reached this point. As the Confederates bunched at the obstruction, he commanded both cannoneers and riflemen to let them have it, and the blast piled them in heaps. For a moment they hesitated in indecision; then they fled. The blue-coats stood up and fired at their vanishing backs.

But in a few minutes the Confederates were back again, this time protected by sharpshooters among the trees and stumps. In their excitement, the Northerners rose high above their breastwork for better aim and thus made perfect targets. The charging lines laid volleys across the parapet tops, too, riddling the defenders. Colonel Rowett, second in the Union command, saw the flag shot down and Corporal Samuel Walker, Company H, 7th Illinois, catch it up, and stand on top of the rampart waving it until a bullet split his skull.

Walker's regimental comrades had, at their own expense, bought $50 Henry repeating rifles a few months before and now rejoiced at the rapidity with which they could plant sixteen shots every minute into the gray ranks that surged and ebbed before them. Once the Confederates broke over the dike at a small sector and, when driven out, carried as prisoner a corporal of the 93rd Illinois. He was using one of the Henry rifles and in the shelter of the forest his captors stared at the wonderful gun. They told him that they would kill him unless he showed them how to work it.

"Go to hell," he replied and went unharmed, to make his way back to the fort during the confusion of the next charge.

Both forts became slaughter-pens—the dead and mangled sprawled over the whole hilltop. The Confederates were coming from so many angles that the ramparts were of small use; some of the defenders had always to stand out in the open to protect the danger points.

IV

As the sun reached one o'clock, a rifle ball knocked Corse senseless and Colonel Rowett, himself wounded, took command. Ammunition was running low and volunteers dashed back and forth between the redoubts over the narrow little footbridge while hundreds of Southerners tried to pick them off.

The Confederates made four major charges between noon and 3:30 P.M., not counting the rushes of small detachments from shelters close to the flanks. One of the attacks brought danger to the precious warehouses. The gnawing of Southern gizzards gave desperation to this raid on the food stores. Rowett barely got Colonel Hann and 500 bayonetmen to the spot in time to turn the Confederates back. In another charge, a lone lieutenant in gray slipped through the line unseen and was discovered racing for the warehouse firebrand in hand. It was too late to head him off. So a Yankee rifleman stood up, aimed at him as at a running rabbit, and got him through the head just in time.

After one early assault the Southern sharpshooters took possession of a pulpit that the Reverend Sylvanus Allen, serving as a private in the 4th Minnesota, had built, weeks before, in a gully. On many a Sunday, Allen had preached from this glory-box, and it angered him now to see the enemy use it as a vantage point from which to kill his comrades. Alonzo Brown of the same regiment observed how Allen trained his rifle on the pulpit and waited. "He gave his attention to it and during the afternoon killed eight rebels in his gospel shop."

From the heights of Kenesaw, Sherman watched the long-continued battle and kept sending messages for Cox to hurry. On the previous day he had sent encouraging signals to Allatoona—one reading, "Sherman is moving in force; hold out," and another, "Sherman says hold fast. We are coming." And, now that the fight was on, he kept the wigwag flags busy with cheering words.

When Tourtelotte's embattled signals read, "We still hold out. General Corse is wounded. Where is Sherman?", Kenesaw answered, "Near you. Hold on. General Sherman says he is working hard for you."

Second Lieutenant John Q. Adams caught the messages on Allatoona and brought them to Tourtelotte, who found them encouraging, as did Rowett, but as the sun crept slowly around to the west, with more men dying every minute, hope began to die, too. Tourtelotte and all but two of his officers were bleeding; some of his best lieutenants were dead. Rowett had only a few officers left standing. Another attack was coming—the worst of all. Rowett, noting how low the ammunition had become, told the 50th Illinois and the 39th Iowa to fire no more, but to draw back and wait with fixed bayonets to stab the gray wave when it broke through. Then he ordered the cannon double-shotted and waited. A bullet bowled him over—his second wound—and Captain Rafferty took command.

Around the unconscious Corse as he lay in the open there was a sudden hush at the command, "Cease firing." The words beat into the General's dazed brain and he came swearing and shouting to his feet, crying defiance. He realized that the next attack would come at any minute. All about the enclosure were muskets that had burst at the muzzle, overheated by too rapid firing. Most of them still retained their bayonets, so Corse had them gathered up and given to such of the wounded as could grip them. Men and guns were propped against the breastwork with the weapons pointing outward. They might fool the enemy into thinking that the defense was still stronger than it was.

The most vulnerable spot in the earthwork was a break made by a ditch, and here a fragment of the 39th Iowa under Lieutenant Colonel James Redfield took its stand. A bullet broke Redfield's leg, but he stayed on, crawling about with his leg dragging, shouting encouragement to his soldiers, who fired so fast that they had to discard their hot pieces for the cooler weapons of dead comrades. A private brought Redfield a chair and he sat in it facing the full blast of the Confederate fire. More balls kept hitting him, but still he sat there, firing his revolver, shouting to his men, till one final bullet shot the last flicker of life out of him and he slid down to the ground, dead at the foot of his throne.

Corse, bracing every spot against the coming onslaught, called surgeons from their bandaging to shoulder muskets at the barricades. He called the sick from the hospital and they wabbled into the line. Isaac R. Russell of the 4th Minnesota was one of them, and although he was so weak that the recoil of his gun kicked him flat on to his back at each discharge, he kept crawling back to pull the trigger again and again—a harder job than dying, which, incidentally, he did not do.

At length, here the Confederates came, jumping over their slaughtered or screeching comrades and, as they drew nearer, forgetting everything and trampling the wounded beneath them. Corse dragged a cannon to an embrasure from which he had cleared the dead, piling them like cordwood on either side. Then he ripped a blanket into wide strips and wrapped them around hatfuls of Minié balls. These he shoved into the gun's throat and sighted the piece, blood still streaming down his face. Then he bent forward, peering, while Sergeant Croxton, himself worse wounded than the general, kneeled by the cannon-butt, lanyard in hand.

When the yelling Southerners were but a few feet away, Corse screamed, "Fire!" and Croxton yanked hard. It was as though he had, by merely pulling a string, jerked the insides out of dozens of men in front of him. The blast was echoed along the parapets of both forts. The whole hill burned flame, charring its attackers. Such of the Confederates as could still move ran for the woods. The battle was over.

Corse, Rowett, and Tourtelotte stood together, dripping gore. They guessed that fully half of their men were down. Both forts were littered with shreds of flesh, bone, brains, bursted muskets, crumpled fatigue caps, bodies in pathetic, ridiculous postures. Cartridge papers, torn and jagged, soaked in red puddles.

There was sniping and sharpshooting after that, but the Southerners were done. By morning, when Sherman was back at his post on Kenesaw, French had gone.

"How is Corse?" signaled Sherman's aide-de-camp, Colonel L. M. Dayton. Quickly the answer came back: "I am short a cheekbone and one ear, but am able to whip all hell yet. My losses are very heavy. Tell me where Sherman is."

Kenesaw replied: "Am reconnoitering. Are you badly wounded? If all is right I want you at Rome." A little later, however, Sherman was less exacting and was telling Corse to remain behind and rest up. "Your head is worth more than a dozen of any I have to spare." When the two men met a few days later and Corse's bandage came off, there was strangely little scar to be seen. Sherman looked at the place, then barked, "Corse, they came damn near missing you, didn't they?" The Confederate General William C. Oates, meeting Corse when the latter was Democratic postmaster of Boston after the war, said that he could see no evidence of either cheekbone or ear having been lost.

In view of another incident, it may be wondered if Corse was not touched with something like hypochondria. Once, before Allatoona, he had fallen on a battlefield and had been borne to the rear, raging and lamenting his inability to carry on. Surgeons stripped him and found only a little blue spot on his leg where a spent ball had landed. However, it is not uncommon for brave men to imagine themselves wounded either more or less seriously than they really are. There can be no doubt of Corse's courage.

For months after the fight, his heroism and the dramatic wigwaggings between his fort and General Sherman were hosannahed in the North. The little battle was called the Second Thermopylae.

On the basis of numbers lost in proportion to men engaged, it was one of the most sanguinary fights in the Civil War. The Confederates left behind 799 of their 3,197, and the Northerners lost 706 of their 1,944 officers and men exposed.

Still, the fight was so small that it might have been forgotten by all save the dull historians if that energetic hymn-writer, Philip Paul Bliss, had not been looking for inspiration nine years later.

v

Throughout the war, Bliss had been at Rome, Pennsylvania, plowing corn and giving singing lessons. He had a wife and at least one child at the time and was not a warlike man, anyway. His father, Isaac Bliss, had been a singer before him, a simple-minded farmer of Clearfield county, where Philip Paul was born on July 9, 1838. The old gentleman sang hymns from the time his bare feet struck the cold floor in the morning until he blew out the lamp at night.

In 1850 a revival swept the region, and a Baptist pastor immersed Philip Paul in the creek behind his father's house. The boy soon became known as a choir singer, both at home and in the neighboring localities where, from the age of eleven, he worked on farms and in logging camps. He received enough schooling to enable him to teach school of winters in Rome, where at the age of twenty he married the daughter of his landlord, having been attracted to the abode by the news that the whole family liked to sing in the evenings.

Soon he had a horse, buggy, and a $20 melodeon and was off, every winter, to teach the rustics how to sing *do, re, mi, fa, so, la, si, do*. Of summers he plowed his father-in-law's corn for $13 a month. In 1864 he composed a ballad, "Lora Vale," and sent it to Root & Cady of Chicago, who issued it with some success at the very time the news of Allatoona's battle was in the papers. Three years later the house received from the young composer his first approach to a hymn. It was entitled "If Papa Were Only Ready." Two verses indicate its quality:

> "I should like to die," said Willie,
>   "If my papa could die, too,
> But he says he isn't ready
>   'Cause he has so much to do;
> And my little sister Nellie
>   Says that I must surely die,
> And that she and mamma—
>   Then she stopped because it made me cry."

"There will be none but the holy—
    I shall know no more of sin;
Though I'll see mamma and Nellie,
    For I know He'll let them in;
But I'll have to tell the angel,
    When I meet him at the door,
That he must excuse my papa,
    'Cause he couldn't leave the store."

It was the success of this dirge, plus the report that its composer back in Pennsylvania was making hardened sinners weep whenever he sang it, that decided Root & Cady to bring Bliss on to Chicago and to make him their chief song-plugger.

Exploitation of songs, in those days, was mainly a matter of conducting "musical conventions" in which small-town choirs, quartets, and soloists would meet and show off. Root & Cady's singers, promoting such affairs, which ran usually from four days to two weeks, taught singing, often at $2 a head for the course, but their principal duty was to see to it that the populace learned the firm's new songs and bought its sheet-music, and that the local churches purchased its hymnbooks.

Throughout four years Bliss worked in and around Chicago for Root & Cady, receiving in return $150 a month and expenses. Then, in 1869, came the event that changed life for the plowboy-composer. Strolling down town in Chicago one Sunday evening with his wife, he heard an evangelist saving souls from the courthouse steps. Stopping to listen, Bliss noted that the singing was weak, and lifted up his voice to show them how it ought to be done. The evangelist noticed him, and when the meeting was over came to him. It was Dwight L. Moody, who promptly hired him to reorganize the music for his revival campaign, then being chiefly waged of noontimes in a theater.

Bliss was off on a new career. The evangelists who swarmed so thickly in the Middle West through those hysterical years after the Civil War learned from him how to employ really catchy tunes. Major D. W. Whittle, another Chicago evangelist—still an amateur at the time —teamed with him and paid him to come as singer on Sunday revival trips to neighboring towns. It was while they were together at Rockford, Illinois, on a Sunday in March, 1870, that Whittle told his singer the story of Allatoona Pass. He said that Sherman's noted signal had read, "Hold the fort; I am coming." Bliss took fire from the tale and that night, back in Whittle's home, where he, Mrs. Bliss, and two little Blisses were staying, he wrote the words and music of the hymn.

Next day he was to lead the singing for Whittle at a service in the Young Men's Christian Association in Chicago and began by writing on the blackboard the verses of "Hold the Fort for I Am Coming." He sang it over and over until the congregation had it by heart. Within a few weeks Root & Cady, for whom Bliss wrote but no longer worked, had it on sale in sheet-music form. It became a national hit and when Moody and Sankey visited England in 1873 it was their principal musical aid in saving the British Isles from hell. Sankey said that shortly after they returned to America, Moody and himself were burlesqued one night by two comedians in a London music-hall, and that the actors were interrupted in their low performance by the simple folk of the galleries, who arose *en masse* and sang "Hold the Fort" until the wretched clowns left the stage.

Having quit Root & Cady for free-lance work among the evangelists and for managing musical conventions on his own account, Bliss began to write songs with greater frequency. For Root & Cady he composed many tunes to the verses, both popular and sacred, which the publishers bought and turned over to him. An appointment to the Sunday-school superintendency of Chicago's First Congregational Church added to his income and allowed him to do more work at home.

As the demand for his hymns grew and as the word came that even in far-off China missionaries were winning coolies from Confucius by singing "Hold the Fort," he turned more and more to the composition of sacred songs. In 1874, while assisting Whittle at a revival in Waukegan, Illinois, he saw so many sinners troop to the altar during his singing of his "Almost Persuaded" that he decided to become an evangelist himself. Making formal surrender to the Lord, he gave over his musical conventions altogether and sallied forth, either alone or with Major Whittle, who at the same time gave up his secular job with the Elgin watchworks and also embraced revivalism as a career. Moody had been urging Bliss to the step for some time, and there was great rejoicing at the news of his surrender.

Thereafter, Bliss was an eminent figure in the Middle West and in the South. One gospel song-success after another was published by Root & Cady or by John Church & Company, the latter specializing in hymnbooks. Church had published *The Charm, a Collection of Sunday-School Music,* by P. P. Bliss in 1871; *Sunshine for*

Sunday-Schools in '73; *The Joy, for Musical Conventions and Church Choir Music,* in '73; and *Gospel Songs, a Choice Collection of Hymns and Tunes, New and Old, for Gospel Meetings, Sunday-Schools, etc.,* in '74. The last of these sold prodigiously and in 1875 Church got Bliss and Sankey to join forces in issuing a compilation of their works under the title of *Gospel Hymns and Sacred Songs.* When this volume outsold all others, they issued *Gospel Hymns and Sacred Songs, Number Two* with the result that Bliss's royalties at the time of his death, on December 29, 1876, totaled fully $60,000, most of which he had given to the cause of evangelism.

Some eight months before his death, Bliss, accompanied by Whittle, visited Allatoona Pass, and climbed Kenesaw to stand where Sherman had stood when he sent the message which, slightly altered, had meant so much to revivalism. "We read the passage concerning the coming of our Lord from Heaven," said Whittle, "knelt in prayer and consecration—and then sang 'Hold the Fort,' looking out upon the distant mountain, looking up at the clear blue sky, and almost expecting that Jesus might then appear, so near He seemed to us that April day."

The following December, Bliss and his wife were in a train riding home to Chicago when it was wrecked in one of the major railroad disasters of the time, at Ashtabula, Pennsylvania. Both were killed.

The Old Judge

"I HAVE to laugh," said George Wharton, the Olympian authority on Thespian history. "I have to laugh when I listen to all this talk about radio announcers, what voices they've got.

"What do they know about real announcing? All they do is put their arms around a thing that looks like a rat-trap on a broomstick, cuddle their cheek against it, and whisper at it."

Mr. Wharton unfolded his hands from upon his stomach and waved them in a brief gesture of despair.

"I'd like to have had about eighty-seven of these modern announcers with me the time, back in 1900, when we had the big announcers' contest in Righeimer's bar. I was said to be on the Associated Press at the time, but what I did most was to judge contests. I never went to bed in those days, stayed up all night and went from one place to another; and wherever there was a dance contest or horse race or singing bout there I was."

A shadow of wistfulness went over the grave face of the Loop humorist, but it was soon gone as he returned to the memory of Righeimer's famous saloon on Clark street, whose long curving bars, French paintings, and shadowy lights once made Carl Sandburg call it, in a poem, "the saloon with a soul."

"Sheridan, the American baseball league umpire, was in there this night," resumed Mr. Wharton, "and he got to telling me and Doc Cunningham, the medicine-show man, about how umpires had the best voices, and we said circus ringmasters were better. So along about midnight we sent our runners to find us a circus announcer and bring him in and see about it.

"There was lots of nice fellows around saloons at midnight in those days, ready to run and get you anything; fine, good-natured fellows.

"Well, anyway this runner—I forget who it was—he was great. He came back with a circus announcer AND— a prizefight announcer. We led 'em up to Sheridan and said, 'Now!'

"Sheridan was ready for 'em, challenged 'em—and after a couple of drinks they took up his challenge—and we got 'em so mad at each other they put up their own stakes—$5 apiece in my hat. Doc Cunningham and I— and somebody else, I forget who—we took seats and pads of paper and were the judges. The floor was cleared.

"Sheridan, he started in giving the batteries of today's game. He started easy, beginning with a minor league game—Indianapolis and Toledo in the American Association. The circus announcer begun on a little old seal act, and the prize-fight man, he announced a couple of flyweights. We announced, too, that we'd grade 'em on three points—voice, diction, and personality—for three calls, but we never wrote anything on our pads but 'oh, pshaw' and things like that. At the end of three calls, we said we couldn't decide.

"The three contestants never tumbled. They got down to business, put everything they had into it. Sheridan finally played his ace, he announced the Giants and the Athletics in a world's series game to 50,000 people at the Polo Grounds, and he announced them so good that the manager of the Sherman down the block, sent a bell-boy over to say his guests upstairs had all woke up and were sore. The noise was awful; people would come in off the street, and never leave; a cop come in to stop it, but he got so interested he wanted to compete. He tried to show how loud and good he could ask a bicyclist where he thought he was goin', so we had to lock him up in the washroom.

"The prize-fight guy played his ace, too. He showed how he'd announce a John L. Sullivan fight. But he over-did himself: his voice broke and we eliminated him. He looked very sad at the $15 lying in my derby right be-tween the judges. Then we got down to a dead heat be-tween the umpire and the ringmaster, and along about nine o'clock in the morning, when Sheridan had been through both big leagues and most of the minors, the circus fellow did a new one. He bellowed:

" 'La-dees and gentel-mun. Let me direct your atten-shun to the most death-defying feat in Christendum; Dare-Devil Daisy doing a eighty-foot dive through loops of concentric fire into a washtub of watah! Are you ready, Daisy! May Gawd have mercy on your soul. JUMP!'

"Then he ducked away, hid his eyes, and moaned, 'Oh! Oh! I can't look! Did she make it?'

"We judges got up and said, 'That get's it,' and I started to hold out my hat with the prize money in it, but Sheridan said, no, that that wasn't announcin'; that was actin', and he wouldn't compete with no damn Louie Mann. So everybody got in a big fight about it and I put on my hat and went home."

The Hill Called
Crowder's Curse

IF Mr. Philip K. Wrigley is the man his father was, he'll turn his baseball yard into a scenic park this winter and have guides showing tourists the spots that were, in October, hallowed all over with history—the history of the 1935 World Series—Tigers vs. Cubs.

And the thing the sightseers will pay most to see is the little hill whereon was pronounced Crowder's Curse, the hill upon which old Uncle Alvin Crowder, the Detroit pitcher, made himself, all one Saturday afternoon, monarch of everything he surveyed.

What the stoop-shouldered old man was throwing during that fourth game, I couldn't make out, even though I sat with 339 other Cherry Sisters of the press behind a net quite close to Uncle Alvin.

But if we couldn't tell whether he was throwing a beach-ball or only a very large cantaloupe, neither could the Chicago batsmen, who were in a still better position to see.

Whatever it was, the aged North Carolina farmer knew what to do with it. He just took it, cocked back his withered old right arm, and aimed it at his friend, Mr. Mickey Cochrane, who knelt a little way off with hands extended as if in prayer. Between the two of them there came and went a lot of the Chicago batsmen, whom their manager,

Mr. Charles Grimm, insists waggishly in calling "big, wonderful young gentlemuns," each of them anxious to hit what Uncle Alvin was throwing. Usually they did hit it, but not for very long nor very far. They seemed to have no more idea about where it was going than whence it came.

A lot of times, during that long Saturday afternoon while Uncle Alvin and his Detroit friends were putting a 2-to-1 scald on the local nine, I would mutter to myself, "That's a slow ball he's throwing. That's what it is," but as often I would be forced to admit, "No; it's too slow for that." Now and then I would think I saw one of his pitches curve a little, but it was probably only the wind doing it.

If it was a sinker he threw, then it was a sinker from gravity, not from sleight-of-hand, and as for Uncle Alvin having a fast one, you may judge for yourself when I tell you that Shirley Temple could have caught him all day with a doily on her left hand.

He made very little, indeed, of the young men who flounced and bounced around him all afternoon, waving bats, running, hollering, jumping up and down. He paid scarcely more attention to the Chicago youngsters than to the handshakes, backslaps, and screeching compliments of the Tiger pups who gazed at him with wondering amazement as he came inching his old flat-feet back from the hill at the end of every inning in his pitching master-piece.

When he was throwing he wasn't whirling his arms in the conventional windmill gestures of young, eager pitchers, nor was he crumpling his insides like an accordion every time he delivered the ball. He just up and aimed like a muzzle-loading old squirrel shooter who was all alone in the backwoods with his prey. And when they made him bat, he never came out scowling ominously at the bat boy and waving three clubs. He just edged out on deck, squatted on his bat like a hen on one egg, and waited until he was needed.

Saturday he got a hit and a run, for his old, cold nose smelled meat in Marse Landis' smokehouse, and he could afford to strain his broken arches a little.

But most of the day he just stood on the hill, with 40,000 people on four sides of him hollering, with telegraph wires singing and radio announcers chattering, and him there on the hill taking it slow, thinking how easy it was to just look at a kid and tell what he couldn't hit, thinking about the flags in the wind, about his feet and about all the places he'd been in his life and all he'd done; then he'd throw one, get it back, and then he'd count the house and throw again.

Once he forgot himself, threw a careless one and saw it go for a home run. You could see him looking in surprise to see who did that. It was another old man, Uncle Gabby Hartnett, the Chicago catcher. Uncle Alvin should have known better, and he did thereafter.

He's been enough places in his thirty-four years to have plenty to think about on an easy afternoon—as a soldier in Siberia, a baseball player in a dozen towns and cities. He's been traded off like a worn-out mule, he'd been sent home with dead arms and bad stomachs, but there he was on the hill last Saturday, winning a world series classic, paying no mind at all to Mr. Grimm's shouts about "big, wonderful young gentlemuns."

Uncle Alvin couldn't be bothered with being a big

"gentlemuns" himself. He's a North Carolina farmer, and down there they raise men to be sensible and to get things done without the fancy adjectives and fine flourishes that distinguish so much of the rest of the South. Your real North Carolinian, he wastes no time bragging about how much his grandpappy lost in the war or how swell everything used to be, he just buckles down to work, building concrete roads or taxing himself for the best state university in the Union or maybe figuring out ways to get city dudes, like Mr. Grimm's gentlemuns, out one, two, three.

The Man the Historians Forgot*

An address at the dinner meeting of the Kansas State Historical Society in the Hotel Jayhawk, Topeka, Kansas, October 18, 1938.

NOT long ago, at a luncheon in Chicago, your president, William Allen White, and I made the discovery that a certain Kansan, who has been dead down among the roots of your grass for more than seventy years, was a mutual favorite of ours—and apparently of nobody else's.

And Mr. White said that I must come out and tell your Society what I had learned about this dead Kansan. I replied that almost everything I had found out had come from your own State Historical Society, and that this dead Kansan would have been forgotten entirely if your Society hadn't been the kind of Society it was—and is— one of the best of all historical libraries, in that it has preserved not only the writings and memoirs and documents of important people, but of the plain people, the masses whom more pontifical and less intelligent historical societies ignore.

The man is your first senator, James H. Lane, who has been crowded out of the schoolbooks and the histories of the nation, and whom various forces might well have eliminated from Kansas' memory, too, if your collections hadn't preserved the record.

Where a man stands in history depends upon who keeps

the record; more than that, it depends upon who lives to keep the record. If you are a favorite of the literary men, the history professors, the clergy, you have a head start toward a place in history. So much of the importance of New England in history is due to its early corner on the literary men, the book publishers, the preachers, the college professors. We are not yet free, as a nation, from the historical prejudices of the New Englanders. For the sake of objectivity there are still too many midland biographers and historians and professors blandly adopting the historical viewpoints of New England—a natural thing, perhaps, for men whose dream it is to be called some day to a full professorship at Harvard.

New England never liked Kansas' most influential citizen of the 1850's and 1860's. That is one of the reasons—there are others—why the schoolbooks of America either have no mention at all of Jim Lane, or merely dismiss him with a few sneering phrases. James H. Lane was a Westerner, an Ohio riverman; he chewed tobacco when he could borrow it; he was divorced; he didn't pay his debts; he took the name of his Lord God in vain—and in stride—he made no efforts to halt the fabulous tales of what his contemporaries described as his "worship at the shrine of Venus," and he only laughed when he was branded as the father of political corruption west of the Mississippi River. Such a man was not to be understood by the elegant authors of New England—the Brahmins who in that day decreed what was good taste in literature.

James Henry Lane came barging into Kansas from Indiana in the spring of 1855, when the fate of the new territory was hanging in the balance between slavery and freedom. Across in Missouri the powerful political machine of Senator David Rice Atchison was dictating the policy of Kansas, and from Washington the greater power of President Franklin Pierce's administration was aiding the proslave forces.

Pitted against these formidable machines was only one organization in Kansas—a little nest of New England Abolitionists in Lawrence—Emigrant Aid Society colonists, whose very "Yankee" presence was enough to drive the border civilization of Missouri to a frenzy. At the head of the Lawrence New Englanders was Dr. Charles Robinson—a physician, not a politician, although he learned something of politics—a cool, calculating man, but without the training to match Atchison and the payrollers of the federal machine in politics.

With him was Old John Brown of Osawatomie, who scorned politicians, and dreamed of blood and war, the sword of the Lord and Gideon. Brown's experience in swaying other men's minds had been limited to a brief career as an unsuccessful wool merchant. He was a child in the hands of the slick politicians on the proslave side, and did commit, in time, a major blunder, the Pottawatomie massacre. Brown, the fanatic, said little and struck hard; Lane, by contrast, said much and killed few. Brown offended, Lane persuaded. Brown was a great failure in Kansas, Lane a great success.

Into Kansas were pouring midlanders, farmers from Illinois, Ohio, Indiana, Wisconsin, Kentucky—men anxious to get land and not caring much about slavery except that they didn't want it where they were, cutting the price of labor.

The bulk of this vote was unexcited, unintense, very cool toward the evangelistic, coercive New Englanders.

It was a scattered vote, with nothing to bind it together to act effectively for Free Soil.

In this extremity of the Free-State population, there appeared Jim Lane, ex-congressman from Indiana, ex-lieutenant-governor, son of the political boss of southern Indiana, wheelhorse of Stephen A. Douglas who was the great politician of the midlands. Lane was a trained and veteran politician, and a gifted one—a master organizer, a highly intelligent man. He came from Indiana where the babies to this day cut their teeth on a poll book, and he proceeded to poll Kansas. A Democrat he had been—and still remained across four more years—a typical Andy Jackson Democrat of the Ohio River regions. But he could count, and he saw that slavery was doomed if the *votes* could be counted. And he was the man to do it— and he did it—and while John Brown comes to the mind when "Bleeding Kansas" is mentioned, it was really Lane who did more than any other one soul to make Kansas free. He knew the tricks with which to overcome Senator Davy Atchison from Missouri; he knew the ruses with which to outlast, outmaneuver the whole administration machine from Washington. It took a powerful politician to meet such odds, but Lane met them. And largely because his methods weren't of the purest, nor his devices of the most admirable variety, the idealists among the New England colonists disliked him. Their leaders resented the slow craft with which Lane absorbed them— the real pioneers—drew them into the main Free-State Party, which he came to dominate and which was ruled eventually by the midlanders, the Westerners themselves.

The New Englanders outlived Lane; they had a stronger hold on the sources of national publicity, on the educational system, and, to a large extent, they wrote Lane out of history, once he was dead—and he *was* dead eleven years after his Kansas career began.

There was a still larger class to want him out of history—the well-born and the well-fed. Lane was for the masses, the ragtag and bobtail, so the conservatives didn't admire him, although they frequently couldn't resist him. And when he was dead and his tremendous personal charm had vanished with the Pied Piper music of his voice—many of those who had followed him tried to fatten their own self-esteem by trying to pretend that he had been nothing but a trivial joke in their lives and in the life of Kansas—an error, I assure you.

Clergymen, as a class, tried to forget him. They had a natural resentment against him because he had made a tool, a jest of their craft. And the clergy, with their close connection with colleges and public education, have been a power in the shaping of history.

One of his greatest strokes of genuis—and he *was* a genius—was to turn the pulpit into the stump at any time, anywhere. It was a thing many men tried to do in that day, but nobody ever did it like Lane. Your Historical Society's collections have word pictures of him at such times—a strange, magnetic man in his middle forties, six feet tall, slender, wiry, nervous, tremendously alive. He burst with vitality—his voice was hypnotic. His hair was long and reckless, and above his ears black locks curled like horns.

There was always the hint of Mephistopheles about him—or of Dionysus, the god of revelry, who loved the plain people and spent his life with them. His eyes baffled men who tried to describe them—they were deep-set and dull when he was quiet; black diamonds, reporters called them, when he was speaking. The touch of genius and its cousin, madness, always there somewhere behind the glaze or the flame.

He had a wide, loose mouth, as mobile as that of a Shakespearean "ham" actor. He was, indeed, an actor, an artist—perhaps a great artist. Astute critics thought him the man of his time who could sway crowds most wholly to his will. A curious mesmerism would flow out from his gestures, his voice, his thoughts, a magnetic overtone that held crowds laughing, weeping, or gritting their teeth, just as he willed. His voice could be a bugle call, or a lullaby.

He had what all great artists have—the power to make the thing they imagine and conceive pass out from themselves and possess other minds.

Again and again is it recorded that Jim Lane's enemies feared to meet him lest they be charmed out of their principles.

If there were time, I could cite you book and verse on the occasions when this vivid and electric man rose before hostile audiences and slowly, craftily, won them to his cause—a Marc Antony oration on the plains. He could rise in front of a crowd where Western rivermen and horsemen stood fingering their revolvers and vowing to kill him, and within thirty minutes he would have them shouting "yea" to a resolution endorsing him for President of the United States.

It is no wonder that the circuit-riding preachers of his day thought him Satan—Satan in coonskin—for he never knew what he wore, any more than what he ate. Rags or broadcloth, he didn't care which, and sometimes he wore a vast black fur coat all summer long and never noticed.

He never bothered to attract men's eyes, it was their ears he wanted. "Give me your ears," was all he asked. He wrote few letters, and left no testaments to history—always a bad thing to forget if you want to live in history. Whenever his political enemies had captured a community with tales of his sins, political or personal, there Jim would go and weave his vocal enchantments again. A camp-meeting suited him best for these returns from Elba. It was his delight to let it be known that he'd be there, then ride up in the night, steal into the back of the singing or bowed congregation, then go forward, kneel, then arise and make public confession of his sins. Slowly the evangelist in charge of the meeting would fade out, and there in his place would be Jim, reciting the human frailties of his life, recounting the gaudy temptations that beset him, picturing the picturesque frailties which struck him down even in the high places he had trod, and winding up by begging the farmers for their forgiveness now and their votes Tuesday. The compliment was one the voters did not care to resist, and in an incredibly short time Jim Lane became the most powerful, influential—and I suspect the most intelligent—political figure in the territory, and by the time statehood came, Jim Lane was the political boss of Kansas—one of the first personal state bosses of a type since familiar all over America.

After Jim Lane was dead many religious people said that he, in rejoining the Methodist church so often, had only used the sacred institution of conversion to gain political power. But it is not so simple and easy as all that, for Lane had a native love of drama; the theatrical elements in churches had a powerful natural appeal to him. There were no theaters on the frontier, and the camp-meeting supplied music, lyric oratory; it was filled with suspense while the saved wrestled with Satan for the souls of the unsaved.

In the 1850's and 1860's there was a simple formula for stump oratory: Get up, say that somebody had said something about you, repeat it twice, and then say "it ain't so." Lane took that common formula, made himself the king of Kansas—he took that formula and went to the United States Senate.

He would get up on a box or endgate of a wagon anywhere on the plains, and cry, "They say Jim Lane is illiterate," and then disprove it by the eloquent and touching statement that his mother had come from Connecticut. He would shout, "They say Jim Lane is a murderer," and then refute it by asking people to remember how he had given his only horse to the ladies of Lawrence to start a public library.

He would begin, "They say Jim Lane is a libertine," and demolish the charge by saying that he had been twenty-one years old before he ever smoked a cigar, swore an oath, or kissed a girl, and that he loved all virtuous ladies, particularly his darling wife. He would croon that so gently that his listeners would forget how his darling wife had left him and gone home to Indiana.

Well educated, cultured, born into the distinguished pioneer family of General Arthur St. Clair, Mrs. Lane had borne with this roving husband for years. She had seen him rush off to the Mexican War; seen him course the state of Indiana making speeches; she had followed him to Kansas, but she had struck at being left in the raw, lonely frontier night after night while he rode the border, drumming up votes for freedom.

So she went back to the Southern culture of the Ohio river town of Lawrenceburgh, Indiana, got a divorce on the grounds of desertion, and thought to marry again. But somehow she didn't. And after two years of reading of the exploits of her husband back in "Bleeding Kansas," she saw that Jim was sweeping through Indiana and Ohio stumping for the Republican Party. And there came a day when the door burst open, and what did she do? Just what Kansas always did—she flew into Jim's arms.

She knew his faults, and she knew he would never change. She knew she was going back with him to a life of loneliness, relieved by nothing but the creditors knocking at the door. She knew that she and the children would go hungry, but she also knew that always, sooner or later, the door would be bursting open and Jim rushing in, his hair flying, his eyes blazing, and his tongue cascading those winning, wooing words again.

The truth of the matter seems to be that Jim Lane seems to have loved life and human beings more than most men are capable of doing. Often he would destroy an enemy politically and then get him a job.

He would make preposterous promises, and then when unable to fulfill them, would tell the outraged victims that he loved them still, and they would forgive him because they had a strong suspicion that it was true.

One of the most dramatic pieces of testimony comes from John Brown, Jr., son of Old Brown, who was more rival than friend of Jim Lane in "Bleeding Kansas." John Brown, Jr., told how on the night before Lane's election as senator by the revolutionary body of Free-State men here in Topeka, Jim came to his room in the Garvey house, asked him to vote for him tomorrow; and when he was told that Brown didn't approve, how Lane poured out compelling oratory, and finally inducted young Brown then and there into a mysterious secret order, a new kind of lodge Jim was getting up—a fraternity which would fight the Missouri devils, fire with fire.

Thirty years later Brown remembered it. He wrote: "Never can I forget the weird eloquence of his whisper as he breathed into my ear the ritual of the first degree of the order, gave me the sign, the password, the grand hailing signal of distress, 'Ho Kansas.' " And Brown recalled how the next morning Lane gave him the emblem of the order, and, after Brown had duly voted for Lane, sent him home to organize his settlements. But that was all. Brown said the great secret order died from Jim's lack of attention.

Lane had *used* Brown, and Brown *knew* it, yet after a third of a century Brown would still say, "But he had my heart and hand then; he has them still. I would not be divorced."

Albert D. Richardson, the famous correspondent of the New York *Tribune*, knew Lane well in Kansas, and summed him up like this, "For years he controlled the politics of Kansas, even when penniless, carrying his measures against the influence, labor, and money of his united enemies. His personal magnetism was wonderful, and he manipulated men like water. He had a sinister face, plain to ugliness, but he could talk away his face in twenty minutes."

Which brings us to a point which years ago I hastily rejected as impious when it first entered my head while reading about Jim Lane: "He could talk away his face in twenty minutes."

Precisely that same thing was said of another man of that time, a man whose career, whose antecedents, whose basic faith was so strangely like Jim Lane's. The man is Lincoln. For Jim Lane was a mixture of Huey Long and Lincoln, and I don't know but that he was more like Lincoln.

For after you have heard all the topsy-turvy tales about Jim Lane, even believed all the half-affectionate, half-scornful anecdotes of his stormy career, even accepted all the stories of his riffraffish scalawagism as partly true, you cannot laugh him off, nor brush him aside. Always a figure of titanic accomplishment comes striding back through the fog. For when everything has been said and done, it was Jim Lane, more than any other man, who made Kansas free soil. He was the organizer of victory; he was the shrewd, scheming politician who knew what weakling to buy and what strong man to inspire. He was the man who called the neighborhood meetings by the side of the road, the mass meetings in churches, the delegate conventions in big halls. When civil war came to Kansas in 1856 and the name "Bleeding Kansas" was on the front page of every newspaper and was the great theme for debates in the United States Senate, it was Jim Lane who led the fighting men, riding the night, directing the raids, the burnings, the stratagems—wily as an Indian, dramatic as General Sheridan in the timeliness of his arrivals on the field.

Kansas laughed about him then, we laugh at him now, but just the same it was Lane who was the head of the executive committees, it was Lane who was chairman in the meeting of that Free-State experiment in revolution, it was Lane who was general of the fighting forces, Lane who wrote the resolutions, Lane who drafted the memorials and appeals for statehood, and when the Free-Soil men of Kansas territory had something formal to present to Congress, it was Lane who was sent to do it.

Lane was a lawyer, but he had small time to practice; he was working for the cause of free soil. He took no time to earn money, because he was too busy with the cause of freedom. He might take a hasty flyer in real estate, then forget about it altogether.

Lane did believe in two things—perhaps only two in the whole realm of life—Kansas and freedom. Born in sympathy with slavery, he became one of the most effective orators and military planners for abolition. Born a Democrat, the son of the Democratic boss of southern Indiana, he became a pillar in the Republican Party of the 1860's. He used every wile and trick in the realm of politics to save Kansas for freedom and the Union for America. There was, I suspect, nothing he would not have done for the Union. The same may be said of Abraham Lincoln.

Only the most innocent of people today still believe that Lincoln saved the Union with beautiful words and tears. It took all the cunning—the almost Oriental type of cunning—in his sharp, deep mind to handle the voters so that the great purpose of his life, the salvation of the Union, might be achieved.

Many of the Jim Lane men, fresh from the battles with Border Ruffians, went to Washington, D. C., in April, 1861, with Jim Lane, to gather around Lincoln in the

White House and protect him from the threats of the Virginia mob.

Yes, when the dramatic hour came for Lincoln, and he was unarmed and practically alone in a Southern city with Secession breaking like the surf around the White House, it was nobody but Jim Lane and a crowd of his war-hardened Kansas Jayhawkers who moved into the executive mansion and sat with their rifles waiting for the Southerners who never came. It is likely a tragedy for the United States that Jim Lane and the Jayhawkers were not still there on an April night four years later.

Lincoln is martyred and goes into history too noble, too exalted to be linked any more with Jim Lane, who committed suicide. Yet, when both were living, Lane may be said to have been President Lincoln's political viceroy in Kansas, and sometimes, perhaps, in the whole regions west of the Mississippi River.

When Lincoln wanted to name a Democrat, Andrew Johnson, as his running mate upon the National Union ticket at the Baltimore convention in 1864, it was Lane whom he probably sent to engineer the delicate deal. Many men later claimed the honor, but the evidence points to Lane. When Lincoln began his campaign for renomination, it was Senator Lane whom he sent to open the drive in the East and in the West. Lane was the keynoter for Lincoln.

Lincoln himself once said that Lane was in the White House almost every day asking for favors for Kansas. The two men understood each other. Why not? Both were born near the Ohio River—Lincoln in Kentucky, Lane in either Kentucky or the Indiana shore—no one can be sure, since he would claim either birthplace, depending upon whether he was talking to a Southerner or to a Northerner. Both were poor. Both received rudimentary educations.

In 1814 Lane's parents left Kentucky for Indiana. Two years later Lincoln's did the same. When Lincoln was nineteen he went to New Orleans on a flatboat and saw slavery in its auction-pen aspects. Lane was in his early twenties when he went to New Orleans on a flatboat, and saw the thing which he later described as having turned him against slavery. A friend left the boat and went up to a plantation to ask for work as a carpenter. The planter drew himself up and said, "I bought two carpenters this morning."

Lincoln in the 1830's was clerking in a general store in Illinois; Lane was doing the same thing in Indiana. Both went to the legislature. Both wanted to be senator and each was disappointed in his home state. Lincoln went to Congress when he was thirty-five, Lane when he was thirty-seven. Lincoln was a soldier in the Black Hawk War, Lane in the Mexican War. Both studied law over the counter in country stores. Both, while young, were favorites of the wild boys of the pioneer civilization. Lincoln was popular with the uproarious Clary Grove gang. Lane was unpopular with his more sedate brothers because he was thick with the wild spirits along the Ohio River levee.

Both were six feet or over—wiry, thin, inexhaustible frontier types. Lane was energetic, Lincoln was lazy. Both loved to talk, and did it well. Both were humorists. Both dominated conversations, meetings. Lincoln was slow, Lane was fast; Lincoln disciplined his mind, Lane did not. Lincoln was great in many ways, Lane can only be

said, as his enemies admitted, to have had greatness in
him.

But both were cut to a familiar border pattern. Each
represented the common change of the Western voter
from Andy Jackson Democracy to the Andy Jackson Re-
publicanism of 1856 and 1860.

Each had been retired after one term in Congress and
had been tossed back into what promised to be obscurity,
until the Kansas issue rose on the political horizon. Lane
went to "Bleeding Kansas" in 1855 and rode the storm
to his great ambition, the Senate. Lincoln bestrode the
Kansas issue in 1858 and rode the storm to the White
House—his great ambition.

Do you wonder then, that Lincoln made Jim Lane one
of the most significant exceptions in his administration?
Lincoln's plan of organizing the federal volunteer army
was to place the patronage, the commissioning of officers
in the hands of the various state governors. But when it
came to Kansas it was not the governor who had the control; it was the senior senator, Jim Lane, and there Lincoln held him, despite the roars of protest from Jim's
factional enemies, and in spite of hints that the injustice
would be corrected, till the end of the war.

And it was obviously with the acquiescence, if not secret
orders of President Lincoln, that the Constitution of the
United States was strained in behalf of Lane. While still
senator, Jim was commissioned a general in the army—
a thing forbidden by the Constitution. The announcements
went forth; Lane didn't resign his seat; he took command
of the Kansas army on the border, led a great raid into
Missouri—a most effective raid from a military point of
view—and in the face of an angry roar of protest, got

away with it. Idolatrous biographers of Lincoln don't dig too deeply into it. It is all a mystery now. Papers were lost, official proof was missing, Jim showed that he had never signed his name as "major general," only as "James H. Lane, commanding brigade"—the thing was glossed over—the Constitution still lived—and the Missouri army had been kept out of Kansas.

And there is another strange story of Lincoln and Lane which the military men, the keepers of West Point tradition, do not explore too deeply. Early in the war, when the federal policy was to deal gently with private property in the South, to return all runaway slaves, and to keep the war aims solely that of preserving the Union, Senator Lane came to Lincoln with a radical plan, not original with him in its generality, but specific with him in its concreteness.

Jim said that the milk-and-water policy of the West Pointers—the General McClellan school—was all wrong. He said the way to whip the South was not to jockey along the Mason and Dixon line, hoping to overawe the Southern states into a peaceful return to the old Union as it was. He said it was time somebody got hurt. He said, "Slavery is the sore shin of the Confederacy; kick it!" He said the way to break secession was to carry the war home to the civilian population. Make it feel the pinch, then it would tell its armies to lay down their guns.

The President was very busy just then keeping radical generals from freeing slaves. He was broadcasting the policy of nonsavagery toward our Southern brothers. But he gave his assent to Jim Lane to organize a great raiding expedition at Leavenworth and invade the South, carry the war home to the people of Arkansas, Louisiana, perhaps Texas, wrecking the resources of the Confederacy. Lane went west across Pennsylvania, Ohio, and Indiana, preaching the new crusade. Every soldier, he said, was to ride a horse like a knight-errant and be attended by a Negro squire—both horse and Negro being picked up along the way.

Volunteers came running. Half-organized regiments in Chicago broke away to join Lane. John Brown, Jr., led a band of volunteers from Ohio to join the man from whom he would not be divorced—and they brought to Kansas for the first time the new marching song "John Brown's Body Lies A-Mouldering in the Grave." All over the midlands voices were saying that Lane was the coming man—the soldier who would win the war. "The Lane policy" was debated in the newspapers. The legions began to gather, a Wild West army, cowboys, Mexicans, Indians, farmers, mechanics, with some immigrant importations—officers from Garibaldi's Italian army.

But Jim Lane's invasion was nipped in the bud, not by the Confederacy but by the Regular U. S. Army clique. The West Pointers, the professionals, the academicians, hamstrung the venture. They bombarded Lincoln and the War Department with the charge that it was nothing but "Jim Lane's Great Jayhawking Expedition." And Lincoln let it die. The army as a whole was more important than any part.

And in all the personal memoirs of the Regular Army men after the war, not one ever had the grace nor the insight to mention the now-obvious fact that what Lane had proposed doing in the winter of 1861-1862 was substantially what William Tecumseh Sherman did in the winter of 1864-1865.

What had been unthinkable when a Kansas politician proposed it was a proper and brilliant stroke of strategy when executed by a professional soldier three years later. "Jayhawking" became a great feat when the regulars performed it. The arming of Negroes had been a mad idea when Lane had practiced it in 1861, but it was a noble measure when the army came to it two years later.

As a matter of fact, Lane had been an instinctive soldier as an Indiana colonel in the Mexican War and as Free-State general in the "Bleeding Kansas" revolution. His Kansas campaigns are models of how guerrilla warfare can be successful with a minimum loss of life. Lane's leadership of the Kansas volunteers in the Civil War was far wiser than the regulars ever admitted. You see, none of the professional people liked Lane—the army men were jealous of him, the clergymen had their natural resentment, the professional literary folk of New England disdained him, the legal profession had scorned him, partly because he ignored the law, and partly because he was reckless with such juries as he faced.

The importance of Jim Lane is not in the law, nor in the establishment of your Kansas institutions, although he was among the first to give land for your state university, nor in the railroads which he helped to bring Kansas—and he pulled wires, coaxed, bullied, intimidated capitalists till they gave the young and sparsely settled state its full share of the transcontinental roads then being built.

His national importance lies not in the fact that he loved Kansas and everything about it, but in the fact that he was among the first of all Americans to see the practical way of establishing a political party which would halt the extension of slavery.

Other men saw it, too, but Lane was among them, at once more visionary and practical than most.

Lane saw that fusion was the way out of the dilemma which convulsed the nation after Stephen A. Douglas' Kansas-Nebraska bill shattered the old system of compromises by which the nation had been held together, half-slave and half-free. His mind was the main forge in which the repellent metals of Kansas' early population were fused into a powerful political party—the one that triumphed in the end. To all intents and purposes the campaign was over within eighteen months after Lane arrived. It could not be crowned for five years to come, but Kansas, as I read the record, was safe for freedom by the autumn of 1856.

Lane organized Fusion, not as a Republican but as a Jacksonian Democrat. He fought to keep Kansas in the control of a party which should be merely Free Soil, neither Republican nor Democrat. What that party should do, where it should go, he left up to old parties back East. Whichever would help Kansas the most got his sanction. He took his story to Senator Douglas, the great Northern Democrat, and, if Douglas had listened to him, the history of America might have been spared the bloody pages of the Civil War. Lane had gone for fusion of Northern interests against the slave South by 1856. Douglas could not see as far ahead and turned it down.

National leader that he was, Douglas had drifted away from the common people; he did not know them in that moment as did Jim Lane. So he remained in the Democratic Party, split it, lost the Presidency. If in 1856 he had been as quick as his former henchman, Jim Lane, to see that the Northern voters would unite in a new party, using Kansas as an issue, he might well have been its nominee in 1856 or 1860, or both. In which case, Abraham Lincoln would have died revered and respected as merely the leader of the Illinois bar.

Stephen A. Douglas did not go for fusion in 1856—he had to wait five years for the light. But eventually he fused, in 1861, at the gates of Civil War.

Although Lane still shouted that he was a Democrat, an Antislavery Democrat, he came out of Kansas in 1856 to stump the Middle West and East for the new Republican Party which had resolved to help Kansas; in fact, its big issue was freedom for Kansas. It drew from the remnants of the Whig Party, but its great appeal was to Antislavery Democrats—the old Andy Jackson men who, on the hard and bony knees of Old Hickory, had learned to hate the Secessionists of the Deep South.

And as the Republicans of 1936 made much of the Liberty League and Al Smith, so did the Republicans of 1856 star Jim Lane—with better results, however. In the campaign of 1856, Lane stumped back and forth across the regions east of the Mississippi, telling the tragic story of "Bleeding Kansas" and begging for all who loved the memory of Andy Jackson to vote for Frémont and against Buchanan.

He was sent into Ohio, a pivotal state, to discredit the Democratic national convention at Cincinnati and to tell the voters that the Democrats were now nothing but the creatures of the rich, the reactionary, the economic royalists and the malefactors of great wealth who had no sympathy with the white laborer and farmer. Lane's great meeting was scheduled for Chicago on the night of May 31—a Saturday night when the workingmen would be free, and the sailors in from the lakes and the longshore-men up from the docks, and the farmers across from the fields. For, make no mistake about it, the Republican Party was a radical, almost a New Deal, party in 1856. It was the masses attacking the classes.

To this great Chicago rally, which Lane was to head-line, came many shouting delegates from Bloomington, Illinois, where two days before Abraham Lincoln had crossed the Rubicon, left the Whigs, and come out for Fusion.

And to add to the hysteria, the telegraph had brought the news that the Proslavery Border Ruffians from Mis-souri had just burned the town of Lawrence, and that in Washington, a South Carolinian named Brooks had clubbed Senator Sumner of Massachusetts to the door of death because Sumner had spoken too violently in his philippic, "The Crime Against Kansas."

Something like delirium—and revolution—was in the air, as the crowd, singing the *Marseillaise*, saw Jim Lane, the hero of "Bleeding Kansas," actually appear before them on the platform.

In the newspapers of the midlands, letters had been appearing from Kansans asking, "Where is Jim Lane? Send him back to us. He is the only man who can save Kansas."

There were wild cheers as Lane was introduced there in Douglas' home town as the man who had renounced his leader and defied him for the cause of human liberty.

It was the moment for Lane's greatest speech, just as two days before in Bloomington it had been the moment for Lincoln's greatest speech up to that time. Lincoln had risen to the occasion with words so eloquent that reporters forgot to take it down and this, his "lost speech," became famous.

Lane, too, rose to the occasion so thrillingly that nothing but confused and hysterical reports were kept. The Chicago *Tribune* said, "Language is inadequate to describe the effect of his recital of Kansas' tale of woes—the flashing eyes, the rigid muscles, the frowning brows."

What people remembered most was how, when the introductions were done, and wild cheers rose and crashed and eddied around him, "he stood there," as a witness tells us, "mouth firm shut, gazing with those wondrous eyes of his into the very heart of the throng. Before he spoke, the fascinating spell of his personality had seized upon the whole vast audience—and for over an hour he controlled every emotion in that great gathering."

That night Jim Lane made Chicago see Kansas as a blackened and charred land, peopled with widows kneeling to kiss the cold white lips of husbands murdered by Proslavery Democrats; he made them see Kansas, which he called "the Italy of America," ravished and despoiled by butchers from Democratic Missouri; he made the large foreign-born population of Chicago roar with rage as he told how the Proslave power had denied the Irish and Germans citizenship in Kansas. He branded the federal administration as abettors of demons and assassins, and he held up that long bony forefinger like a tremendous exclamation point as he cried, "Before God and these people, I arraign President Franklin Pierce as a murderer."

As he ended, pandemonium took the scene. Lane had let loose havoc and the dogs of war. Gamblers threw their pistols onto the stage, begging Lane to take them to Kansas and use them; sailors threw their wages onto the platform at Lane's feet; staid businessmen tossed in their purses; it is said newsboys cast their pennies up; women wept, men wept, the people milled around the platform singing, shouting.

They were the Commune that night, and Jim Lane was Danton, and it was all very well for our record as a safe and sane nation that the American Tuileries were 800 miles away.

Nor was it a passing craze of a single night. Next day it was found that $15,000 had been pledged to raise aid for the revolutionists in Kansas, and that men were volunteering to go and fight the Proslavery armies which were backed by the federal power in the bleeding territory.

And some of the emigrants who did go from Chicago went with bayonets. And when the largest body rolled overland through Iowa and down into Kansas it was called "Lane's Army of the North." Not "settlers," not "Fortyniners," not "emigrants," but an "army." It was the overture to the Civil War, and Lane was waving the baton. He was at the army's head till he neared Kansas, then he spurred on in advance, making one of the best rides in the history of the Wild West, riding so hard that his companions—one of them Old John Brown, of Osawatomie—fell by the wayside, unable to keep up with this strange leader who never seemed to sleep nor eat but to feed himself upon eloquence. Lane never took alcohol, they say, and I believe them, for, after all, what could it have done for him?

The story of Jim Lane's return to Kansas is in your records—how, to spread terror among the Border Ruffians, the enemy, he magnified the size and number of "Lane's

Army of the North"; and how, to encourage the all but beaten Free Soilers, who had begged for his return, he broadcast the whisper, "Look for Captain Cook on a white horse."

Everybody knew that Captain Cook would be Jim Lane, for whom the government held an indictment for high treason, if not a price on his head.

The amazing propaganda that he spread did cow the Proslave bands, and it did inspire the Free Staters to a superb burst of activity, with men marching through the night to bombard enemy blockhouses, burn and shoot. And it was a matter for cheering when through the darkness the marching men heard, "Here comes Captain Cook," and turned to see it was Old Jim, his eyes afire.

This was the campaign which swept the border, and settled the fate of Kansas so far as armed force was concerned, and it is known elsewhere than in your state. But what is not generally remembered is that Jim Lane's most sensational speeches in Chicago, Cleveland, and other midland cities, a month previous, were one of the most vital factors in the national financing of the Republican Party.

Organized wealth and the conservative powers were against the young party. Its supporters were poor. But in the money which orators like Lane collected for the relief of Kansas, came the sinews for the new party. Most of the states organized Kansas committees, and these had a central committee in Chicago, which united the workmen, since the chief issue of the campaign was "Kansas—Shall it be free or slave?" It was thus an easy matter to unite the moral and philanthropic cause of Kansas relief with the Republican campaign. Every speech made for Free-Soil Kansas was a Republican speech.

Without Lane's inflammatory speeches in the midlands, would this money-raising device have been so effective? Probably not.

We must have done with this intriguing man. A word will wind him up. He went to the United States Senate; he was a power in the renomination of Lincoln in 1864, in the new Fusion which Lincoln decreed for that campaign, the fusion of Republicans and War Democrats in the National Union Party, and when the war was over and reconstruction at hand, Jim went with President Johnson for reconciliation toward the South. Not so prominently as some, but enough to set the Abolitionists and his old factional enemies, the New England Black Republicans, calling him a traitor to his party.

Was he gravitating back toward the Democratic Party, as was Johnson and so many of the conservatives who had been close to Lincoln? Probably so.

When Senator Lane voted to support President Johnson in the fight with the Radical Republican Congress, he heard that Kansas had risen against him, and that where he had been yesterday boss, and king, now nobody would speak to him. He went with the Lincoln program of mercy toward the South—and it wasn't popular. He also heard himself denounced and investigated by senators on the charge of having taken cash bribes from Western contractors.

He came home to Kansas and shot himself through the head, and to his enemies who lived after him and had their hand in the writing of history, this was enough to prove him guilty. His friends, in the main, were the inarticulate masses, who had nothing to do with textbooks. But to the neutral mind which studies Lane's whole life, these easy explanations for his death are not convincing.

The man had lived the last eleven years of his life facing down charges as serious as these. Indeed, Jim Lane in 1858 had outfaced and lived down the charge that he had murdered his neighbor in a fight over a waterhole. He had walked the streets of Lawrence an outcast after that catastrophe, yet within three years had come back to be elected United States senator and to become king of Kansas.

He had always thrived on accusations against himself, and had climbed by turning them to his own account. Was he devastated because Kansas disapproved him politically? Hardly that. He had met political midnight many times before, and with a whirlwind campaign had turned it once more into dawn.

His whole life belies the charge of bribery, for he never cared for money. It was not his medium of exchange. He had never taken time to collect it. It didn't interest him. What could it bring him compared to the things his silver tongue could bring? He was a genuine artist, and genuine artists are fools where money is concerned. Jim Lane would rather bind fifty farmers in the spell of his oratory than win a fat fee arguing a case before twelve jurymen.

The hunger of his own children, the gauntness of his own frame are the witnesses against the charge that after a life of ignoring money he suddenly sold out for a few thousand dollars.

No; as I read the record of his life, Jim Lane shot himself because with the end of the Civil War, he saw his whole world gone, his era dead, his age vanished. He was the pioneer, the adventurer, the restless hunter for new horizons, and the glories of that era had vanished. He was a revolutionist, and the revolution had been won and was thenceforth to be in the hands of the corporation lawyers. He was a fighter, and the war was over.

After Appomattox, America had set its feet in the path of the merchant, not the politician; in the way of the advertising agent and the industrialist, not the spellbinder on the newly cut stump. And Jim Lane probably saw it.

In 1866 he came home and looked at Kansas. Was this fat and peaceful land the place where only ten years before he had been Captain Cook on the white horse riding in the glare of burning barns? Were these quiet business-men who were now meeting in chambers of commerce the ragged boys who had manned the rifle pits upon which he stood firing them to bravery with his oratory?

He had had a lot of fun, and now he couldn't have it any more. He had slept at Lincoln's door in a night of peril with his naked sword, literally, across his knees, and now Lincoln was gone.

He had never been the best father in the world, but he had been tender with his children whenever he thought of them, and, after all, few fathers had taken their chil-dren to see Lincoln as often as he. Kansas didn't need him any more: it was free, the Negro was free. What was there to make speeches about now?

Jim Lane saw that the rules had changed; as William Allen White put it, "Jim Lane saw the counters were different," and all at once he realized that Kansas and America were going to bore him.

Here was a civilization with which he could not cope. In the whole of the United States there was now, henceforth, no fuel for the great fires within himself to feed upon.

Imagination can picture him, standing there, and remembering back, recalling, now, a place often mentioned in the religious litanies of his Calvinistic boyhood, a strange, dread pit in which the fuel was promised to be everlasting. This might be the place for him now?

He would go and see.

"*Keep Movin*'"

SATCHEL PAIGE, probably the most remarkable pitcher in the history of baseball, explains very simply the durability which has preserved him through sixteen years of Herculean hurling. He has pitched around 125 games a season, with his seasons lasting twelve months, thanks to the freedom with which he flits between the temperate and the tropic zones—the United States all summer, Latin America all winter.

"I was born with control," he says. "I take two awful hot baths a day; I keep movin' all the time on the diamond—and I eat nothin' but fried food."

Six feet, three inches, weight 175 (he has gained four pounds in twelve years), age thirty-eight, long, limber, lean, and easy of carriage, Mr. Paige is blessed with the temperamental repose of his racial fellow-star, Stepin Fetchit. Ever since 1924, when he came out of Alabama to become the blinding star of the Negro baseball world and the distant but prodigious legend of the white baseball world, which sees him only in barnstorming times, Mr. Paige has been a curiosity, a show, a fabulous and mysterious legend.

Nobody who ever saw him ever forgot him, so dramatic is his slim indolence on the mound, his apparent laziness, which lasts only till he throws the ball at his catcher. The progress of that ball is historic, for it travels as no ball, not even Dizzy Dean's or Dazzy Vance's or Walter Johnson's, ever traveled.

It is like lightning striking out of a sleepy summer-day cloud. It strikes and it is a strike.

Baseball experts and stars in the white major leagues have said Satchel Paige would be the greatest pitcher in the game if the big leagues admitted Negro players to their ranks. Mr. Paige, himself, is absolutely confident he could win thirty-five games a season in either league, for he has, upon barnstorming occasions, made monkeys of some of the best batsmen in the American and National leagues. Once when Joe DiMaggio was preparing to make his tryout with the Yankees, he batted against Paige in Coast winter games, and, after many fruitless efforts, did manage to get a hit. He said, "Now I know I'll make good with the Yanks—I got a single off Satchel Paige."

Sixteen years Mr. Paige has been going, playing in one-day stands all over the nation. He has pitched in Mexico, in South America, Central America, Hawaii, Japan, in the West Indies. He is the great vagabond of the game, the great itinerant, striking out his fourteen to seventeen men a game in Caracas, San Domingo, New York, Los Angeles, Seattle, Mobile (his birthplace), mowing them down anywhere, everywhere. [His record is 19.] And now, at thirty-eight, with sixteen seasons behind him, he is on a barnstorming tour with the Kansas City Monarchs and pitching, by contract, from three to six innings six days a week.

That long, thin right arm of his is, therefore, the most astonishing piece of mechanism in the annals of baseball.

"Why does it last so good?" he repeated the other day as a questioner pinned him down. "Because I take care of Number One—and Number One is here"—his long forefinger made a semicircle around his stomach and back muscles. "I take care of the muscles 'round here. That gives me balance. That keeps my arm from getting strained, ever. Keep your back strong and your stomach down and you'll have balance—and balance is what you need out there on the hill.

"Why, I can stand on one foot for thirty minutes like a statue in the park."

He rocked easily back and forth in a spring office chair and talked slowly, easily, and his questioner forgot all about the similarity to Stepin Fetchit, for Paige is anything but slow when he talks about baseball, anything but lazy when he gets down to the secrets of conditioning.

He is a shrewd and serious man when he analyzes his durability.

"They say too much exercise will get you," he said, his drawl gone, his eyes intent and sharp. "Now, I never did see where it got you. I see where it makes you, that's all. I keep movin' from the minute I step on a ball field. I never do sit still till I come back after the first inning. Before the game, I start fielding bunts, then I hit to the infield, then I chase flies, or work out at third, but I never do throw till ever' muscle, ever' single one, is all loosed up. People tell me to sit, rest, not work so hard. They say I'll break a finger. I tell 'em my hands take care of themselves. I could play the infield if I didn't pitch.

"When I get all loosed up, I get me a catcher and warm up, but I never do throw hard till I'm sure ever' little muscle is fine and free. I never did throw a ball in the last thirteen years without EVER'thing was loose and ready.

"I never throw 'em cold. NO day.

"I take a bath, hot as I can stand, when I get up in the morning and then I take one hotter'n that after a game— so hot nobody else could stand it. Near boilin', that's how hot I take it. And it has kept my arm from ever gettin' sore, and it's kept my arm alive. Just as good today as it ever was.

"And then I keep movin', like I say, for an hour before I start to pitch. I bend and whirl and loose my muscles up before I ever do throw hard at all.

"You can eat anything if you keep movin'. Keep movin' and the fat will never settle anywheres. Fat can't catch hold on you if you keep movin'."

Satchel's long fingers stroked across his stomach like a pianist dusting a Steinway.

"I never do eat anything but fried food," said Mr. Paige. "No boiled food, jus' fried.

"In those Latin countries I ate ever'thing. I ate their fruit and I drunk their water while all the other American players on my team stood around waving their hands and hollering, 'Typhoid,' and things like that. But I never did get it, one minute.

"They liked me on the coacher lines when I was playing in Puerto Rico, and I liked them. I got so I could speak some Spanish, and I'd get off up into the jungles sometimes to see what it was like. Once we had political trouble and Sam got us out, but most of the time it was nice. It was more comfortable than any other of them Latin countries, because Sam owned it." (Sam is, of course, Uncle Sam, in Mr. Paige's language.)

"I haven't had a cold in twelve years, either. I never do come North till June or July, and for the last four years I've been stayin' in Puerto Rico in winter. Where it's warm, I like to pitch. I got me in Chicago this week the first overcoat I've had in five years, for I'm stayin' in America this winter. Can't tell what baseball would be like with all this war talk in the West Indies."

Mr. Paige's interrogator said, "You've traveled more than any other professional athlete. I suppose you've been in all the states of the Union?"

Satchel rocked reflectively a few moments, then decided, "All of 'em but two—Maine—and Boston."

"With that fast ball of yours, how do you find catchers?" he was asked.

"I'm the easiest man in the world to catch," he said. "I jus' pick up catchers catch-as-catch-can if I'm travelin' without a team. All he has to do is to show me the glove and hold it there. I'll hit it. I can knock a box of paper matches out of a man's fingers at sixty feet. They can hold out two bats, one six inches above the other, at the plate, and I'll throw a ball between them from the pitcher's mound.

"All a catcher has to know about me is when I'm throwin' my beeline ball and when I'm throwin' my jump ball. I throw both with the same overhead motion. Only the bee-ball goes off with my fingers on the smooth hide and rides on the level, while I throw my jump ball with my fingers across the seams. That makes it jump four to six inches.

"Three years ago I threw my first curve. Before that I never did bother about it for my fast one was enough. Then I thought I'd save my arm for my old age and I began slow curves and a knuckle ball. My curve is never fast. I never break it off. Might crack a bone in my wrist.

Just a slow curve to fool 'em. The batters can't believe it from me. They hear about my speed and they can't believe the curve when they see it. I use it for strike three when I have him three and two. I got seventeen strikeouts in one day this summer on men waiting in that three-and-two spot for a fast one and then gettin' a slow curve.

"I can get that curve right in the heart as good as my fast one."

Mr. Paige thinks it is not only speed and a change of pace that fools batters; he throws fast balls from three angles, overhand, side-arm, and underhand.

He pinched his arm as he explained it. "I use three sets of these here little biceps. Overhand uses one, way out sideways uses another, and up from down there still another one. That's another reason my arm never does get tired."

Unlike other ballplayers, white and Negro alike, Mr. Paige is not superstitious. He loves to strike out the first batter. In fact he loves to strike out all batters, but particularly the first four. "That gives the rest of 'em the idea," he grins.

"I throw the first time high to each batter as he comes up, and I watch how he lunges at it. From then on I know where he wants it and what he can't do."

In an hour's talk, Satchel knocked wood only once and that was when he said: "I never hit but two men in sixteen years' pitchin'. That was one day in 1932 in St. Louis when I lost control. It really scared me, for with my speed I might kill somebody.

"It has been thirteen years since I dusted a batter. I

don't have to, and I don't want it on my mind. Sometimes hitters think I'm dustin' 'em when I throw my first side-arm ball up there. It comes from so far out that they think it's coming right at 'em. But it ain't; it's coming right over the plate, and they see it too late."

He was asked: "Of all the batters you've faced, who was the hardest to fool?"

Like a flash the answer came, "Charlie Gehringer of the Detroit Tigers. Yes, him. When they hit flat-footed they're the best hitters, and he sure stands there flat-footed. Joe DiMaggio is good, but that Gehringer he's REAL good."

Mr. Paige has pitched no-hit no-run games in his time, the most recent in Detroit, but he doesn't try for them. In fact, he likes to let a runner or two get on base and then strike out the side with the ball whistling and the crowd screaming.

Once pitching in a series between Negro All-Stars and white All-Stars, he had won his game and was on the bench next day when the whites filled the bases with no-body out. He looked up at Candy Jim Taylor, his manager, and, twiddling his glove, said: "You want the side out, Candy Jim?"

A nod, and out to the mound, walking as slow and confidently as did Alexander the time he came on and struck out Lazzeri for the all-time climax of World Series excitement, now came the great Satchel.

As he left the bench, he said to Taylor, "Candy Jim, you hold up a finger for ever' out I get. I'll look over to keep up on things, and you just stand there and sign me where I'm at. I sometimes forget how many's out."

Then he went out and threw three times and saw Candy Jim put up one finger. He threw three more and Candy Jim held up two. He threw three more and Candy Jim made it three and the crowd made it Niagara.

Nine times the lightning had struck from out of that slow summer-day cloud that is Satchel on the hill.

"De Lawd's" Only Friend

"DE LAWD" has lost his only friend—"Gabe."

Sam Davis, who played the Angel Gabriel in *The Green Pastures* is dead—the second "Gabe" to die since Marc Connelly's great play began its career. And the tour continues. Another Gabriel experiments with the Trumpet of Doom and sees to it that the angels have the proper wing-ointment.

But "De Lawd" will, in all probability, never have another friend like Sam Davis.

Wesley Hill, the first Gabriel, was more famous than Sam Davis. Hill created the role, and, at the time he was killed by a taxicab in New York, was a prime favorite on Broadway. People said there would never be another "Gabe" like Hill. His face was droll, his manner was humorous. He made Gabriel a most entertaining fellow.

But Sam Davis—just a Negro actor of the varieties without any special preparation for so difficult a role—stepped into the part and made, what was to me, a far better realization of a Recording Angel such as Mr. Connelly had in mind. Where Wesley Hill had been a sort of star all by himself, almost a minstrel interlude, Sam Davis was an artist, humbler—a part of the play. Sam made "Gabe," the friend of the Lord God—the sympathizing, understanding, intimate—the only person in the immeasurable reaches of Paradise who comprehended God's woes. All the other celestials, prophets, angels, cherubs, stood in awe of the Most High—Sam's respect was that of admiration and love.

When Hill's "Gabe" surreptitiously practiced on the Judgment Trump it was for a laugh. When Sam Davis' "Gabe" did it, you felt that it was nothing but a preparation for the blast which would set the Lord free. The Lord was in trouble. He had made Man, populated the earth with humans—and they had gone bad. They worried God with their sins. They deviled Him day and night. He didn't know how to reform Man.

Well, Sam Davis knew how to get God out of trouble. Just blow that horn and all would be over. Wipe out the earth and its denizens! Summon 'em to the Bar of Judgment. Let 'em take their medicine!

"De Lawd" would never let Sam blow it. Sam went to the end of the play serenely contemptuous of Man as a low trouble-maker: always politely anxious to end sin with the toot that would finish Time and Strife.

I shall never forget Sam's "Gabe" at the end of *The Green Pastures*. "De Lawd" was in pain. He had turned from a God of Wrath to a God of Mercy. He was perceiving that He must go down to earth for another attempt to save Man. He must go and die as an object lesson to sinners.

Sam's "Gabe" didn't understand the divine necessity. All he knew was that the great Man, whose companion, confidant, and attendant he had been, had a new woe on His face. Sam wanted to help Him.

"You look a little pensive, Lawd," he said. "Have a seegar, Lawd?"

"No, thanks, Gabriel."

Sam edged anxiously toward where "De Lawd" was sitting, staring into space.

"You look awful pensive, Lawd. You been sittin' yere, lookin' dis way, an awful long time. Is it something serious, Lawd?"

"Very serious, Gabriel."

Then Sam leaned forward and asked, in a low, compassionate voice, "Lawd, is de time come for me to blow?"

"Not yet, Gabriel."

Sam gave it up. He couldn't understand why the Most High let Himself be harrowed by those no-good humans.

When Wesley Hill asked that question it made audiences smile, but when Sam asked it, people wept. Wesley was a Divine Court Jester. Sam was God's friend, and— who knows?—he may be really that today.

They Didn't Want
"Free Enterprise"

IT will be surprising if any commencement address this June stirs up as much talk as did Laird Bell's at the University of Chicago convocation.

A lawyer of Supreme Court stature, to say the least, a rich man of genuinely liberal mind, a creature of conscience, Bell is always worth listening to, and never more so than when he stood up there in the Midway pulpit and told the young graduates to be off, now, on the trail of fun, adventure, and achievement rather than on the rockless road of security and standardization.

He told them there had been too much talk, the past thirteen years, about security. They shouldn't, however, swallow all that businessmen were claiming for free enterprise. He reminded the young people how these same businessmen only a few years ago were bawling for the federal government to come and save them from the panic of 1929. And how, when asked by the federal government to draft a plan for their own salvage, they created a NRA Blue Eagle which was stuffed with regulations.

Admit all that, he said, and you still have ample grounds for dedicating yourself to free enterprise rather than security. "Be like the pioneers" was the burden of his song. Rely on yourself! Plunge spiritually into such adventurous wildernesses as the world, today, may present!

Bell was restating, with eloquence, one of the great romantic beliefs of America—the idea that the land was wrested from the catamount and the red devils by successive waves of bold men who, scorning dull, drab Eastern conformity, sought perilous self-determination on Western frontiers.

A noble theme, indeed, but one which would have made the pioneers' eyes bat if they could have heard it, for what sent them westward was, plainly enough, not a hunger for danger but for security.

For every Daniel Boone who wanted to go it alone, there were 100,000 settlers who were entirely too practical to fool around with that kind of free enterprise. They came into the wilderness hunting security from poverty, from landlessness, from unemployment, and they came whooping for a kind of paternalism that would have frightened Henry Wallace.

They didn't say to Uncle Sam, "Stand back! We'll handle our competitors!" Instead, they yelled for him to send federal troops and eliminate the Indians. They made the wilderness trails resound with their howling for free land. When the federal government gave it to them at only $2 an acre, they grumbled. When it cut the price to $1.25, they stormed. And it is significant that the President who, until then, was the westernmost of all our Chief Executives, Abraham Lincoln, finally got it for them, scot-free.

But it is more significant, now, when the Rooseveltian concept of security is being challenged, to remember that the most self-reliant and individualistic Americans of our history, the hardy pioneers, believed that they could receive lavish federal aid without losing their souls. They had so little fear of character-decay that they forced Uncle Sam, as the Beards so well point out in their *Basic History of the United States*, to give them internal improvements, canals, harbors, locks, wagon roads, and in addition to their free homesteads, enough more land to prime the pump for railroad builders. Great numbers of them, led by Henry Clay, joined with their fellow-travelers, the industrialists, to demand pap in the form of a high protective tariff.

As a matter of fact the worship of free enterprise began not in pioneer America but in the dawn of the big corporations after the Civil War. That it was a different kind of free enterprise from the kind the pioneers had enjoyed was something the corporative evangelists failed to mention.

Back of the pioneers were the colonists who came to the Atlantic Seaboard expecting security from poverty, from religious oppression, from the uneasy life.

Paul Scott Mowrer, the journalist-scholar, looked deeply into the causes of America's settlement during his long years abroad, and concluded that more Old World peasants migrated to get good hunting and fishing than to get religious freedom.

From travel books about the New World, from the cagey promotors of land companies, and, later, from Cooper's best-selling novels, British, Irish, Scotch, German peasants learned that the killing of game for food was a sure thing all the way from Massachusetts to Florida and points west. Advertisements told them, in effect, that they could step off the boat, shoot a gun in any direction, and bring down at least three turkeys, four deer, and a goose.

Also, they could lower a bent pin into any stream and come up with nothing less than a sturgeon.

This sounded like security to peasants who had never had enough meat in their lives and whose brothers had been hanged for poaching. No sheriffs to chase them for snaring a hare? That was practically Nirvana.

The truth of the matter is that these peasants had spent so much of their lives dodging or fighting the constables who wanted to jail them for debt, or gibbet them for praying to the wrong dominie, or draft them for the stirring perils of professional soldiery, or to impress them into the Homeric life of a seaman, that it could hardly be said that they came to America seeking adventure.

If that was what they wanted, they'd have stayed home.

Not in "The Green Pastures"

MARC CONNELLY, hunting a new "Lawd" for his resumption of *The Green Pastures*, stopped in town the other day and got to talking about the late Alexander Woollcott.

"Sam Adams' biography of Alex [*A. Woollcott: His Life and His World*] doesn't complete all the stories it brings up," said Marc, who with Woollcott, George Kaufman, and Franklin P. Adams was the center of that band of wits that gave New York's Algonquin Hotel so literary a flavor.

"The biography recites many of the squabbles between Alex and Harold Ross, editor of the *New Yorker*, but it doesn't tell one of the incidents that prompted Alex to call Ross 'a fourth-rate man.' One day Ross came over from his *New Yorker* office to have lunch and said he was going to see such and such a play with Woollcott that night. I asked why that show. It was a flop.

"Ross said, 'That's enough. Woollcott has taken me to three flops in a row the last two weeks. I'm going to tell him I can't go.'

"What he told Woollcott I don't know—he had to work or was out of town or something. Anyway, he and I were eating in the Algonquin that evening when Woollcott came in and was in the act of sweeping off his cape to sit down at a table when he saw us. He glared at Ross, put his cape back on and swept out.

"Ross said, 'I've got to square this somehow.' I said, 'I'll fix it.' I got a telegraph blank and wrote this wire to Alex: 'I'm in a bit of a jam. If anybody asks you where I was tonight, say I was with you. Signed, Harold Ross.'

"I handed it to Ross and said, 'Why don't you send that?' To my surprise he did. It drew the 'fourth-rate man' reply from Alex."

Connelly corrected the idea that Woollcott had coined the famous epigram about Moss Hart's tree—an idea that has become very general.

"It was Wolcott Gibbs, instead," said Connelly. "Ross asked his drama critic, Gibbs, to do a profile on Moss, whose success as a playwright was a big Broadway topic. Gibbs went down to Hart's new estate in New Jersey and was shown a magnificent elm which Moss had had transplanted to a spot just the right distance from a window.

" 'H-m-m,' said Gibbs, 'that shows you what God could do if He had money.' "

This is not the first of the stories erroneously attributed to Woollcott. He himself was, as his readers and radio listeners know, careful to tell where and when he got those of his anecdotes he didn't invent. From years of friendship with him I knew of only one he borrowed without credit and in this case he was meticulous in announcing that he had done so.

That was one that I reported to him, by letter, in 1938. On a boat approaching Hawaii, an extremely self-satisfied old sugar planter—scion of those missionaries who went to the islands to do good and did well—was regaling listeners with his delight at getting back from the "main-lund," as feudal Hawaii calls the United States. Someone asked him where he had been vacationing on the vulgar mainlund, and he said, "Chandler, Arizona." Somebody else, to make conversation, asked him if he had seen any of Frank Lloyd Wright's buildings there.

"No," said he, pursing his lips haughtily, "there are two men on the mainlund I despise: Franklin D. Roosevelt and Frank Lloyd Wright."

He was asked why those two.

"Because," said he, staring loftily out to sea, "Franklin D. Roosevelt has taken the best things from the best people and I could never forgive Frank Lloyd Wright for shooting Harry Thaw."

I hurried this revealing piece of Bourbonism off, by airmail, to Frank Lloyd Wright, who wasn't at all surprised, since an astonishing number of people, across the past forty years, have confused him with that other celebrated architect, Stanford White, who was shot and killed by Harry Thaw. I also sent the story winging to Woollcott at his island in Lake Bomoseen, Vermont, and got back word that, the minute he read it, he phoned the White House, asked to come down, was urged to do so, as he always was, hopped a train, boiled in on Franklin D., and told him he couldn't avoid re-election in '40, for here was the kind of opposition facing him. Then he told the story saying that it had happened in a conversation between the sugar planter and himself on a train.

He said the President laughed helplessly, and I do know that Woollcott stayed at the White House that time for, it must have been, three weeks. The truth of the matter was that the story meant much more to Roosevelt as happening to a friend than to someone of whom he had never heard.

Mention of Hawaii reminded Connelly of how one night in Hollywood a group were taking turns describing the damage the white men had done to island natives across the world, wrecking their simple pleasures and debasing their primitive characters with crass commercialism.

"Yes," spoke up Moffatt Johnson, the British actor, in a heavy burr, "they dom near ruin't Scutland."

King of the Bull Pen

THE other day a fellow-alumnus of Swarthmore College said to me, "Did you know that Eisenhower was on that West Point baseball team you fellows played in 1913?"

Since baseball is one of the few things I ever remember about college, this revelation came with shattering impact. I remembered everything about that West Point game, all but the names of the Army players. We hadn't bothered about who they were. We pitchers studied them intently only to discover each hitter's weakness.

So, Eisenhower had been one of those Army hitters! To discover this, thirty-two years later, made my head wheel, and for five days I have done nothing but sit around and think how near I came to striking out Eisenhower.

I have looked in his biographies—*General "Ike" Eisenhower*, by Delos Lovelace; *General Ike, a Biography of Dwight D. Eisenhower*, by Alden Hatch; *Eisenhower, Man and Soldier*, by Francis Trevelyan Miller; and *Born to Command, the Story of General Eisenhower*, by Helen Nicolay—but am really not surprised to find there no mention of that game. They tell how Eisenhower, Class of 1915, played football and baseball but mention nothing specific in the way of diamond dramatics. This game against Swarthmore was, of course, too small a thing to have been recorded, but to me it now looms large indeed.

I try to be modest about it, but I keep wondering if it is too much to say that once I came as near as Von Rundstedt to fanning Eisenhower.

Up to that spring day when we journeyed from Philadelphia to West Point I had been merely a substitute pitcher, the one who pitched to our boys in batting practice and then repaired to the bull pen to keep warmed up in case our varsity pitcher, Newt Tarble, should falter. The only trouble was Newt had never faltered sufficiently, and I had become known as "King of the Bull Pen." I had been warmed up for two years but had never got into a game.

At the end of our Saturday games, I'd be the weariest man on the squad.

As we started this game against the Army, I felt in my bones that this was to be THE day. Today I'd get the call; now, I felt the law of averages would catch up with Tarble and let me get in.

So confident was I that I began warming up in the bull pen even before we, as visitors, went first to bat on the diamond that lay in one corner of the great parade ground. And I worked down there steadily as the game progressed, never sitting down to rest, no matter how piteously my catcher complained of the heat. No word of restraint came down to me from the bench. I was used to that. The coach had forgotten me for two years already.

The game was a tight one, and I watched it intently while I worked, although it was getting pretty hard to see, along about the seventh inning, because my swinging, lunging spikes dug deep into the ground slowly lowering me into a hole as I put everything I had into the out-curves, drops, in-shoots and out-drops as deliveries were called in 1913. I even changed my delivery in the eighth inning from side-arm to overhand, because Tarble threw side-arm and when I should be called, I would the easier baffle the Generals with a ball coming up from a new angle.

The ninth inning passed with the score tied; and as the tenth started, I had burrowed so deeply that I was practically throwing to the catcher by sound, and I worked faster and faster as the Army hitters got men on. Tarble was weakening, and only sharp fielding by our boys saved him.

Surely the coach wouldn't be fool enough to risk that worn-out old man the next inning. I tightened my belt, hitched my socks, loosened the wet rag of a uniform on my shoulders, and began imitating Christy Mathewson, the fabulous New York Giant pitcher, who was a demigod to most boys of that time. While our batters went down, one, two, three, I rehearsed my forthcoming entrance avidly. When the call would come, I would go striding across there to the mound, with all of Mathewson's lofty arrogance, my every motion saying, "Now, all this nonsense will stop," and then I'd strike out three men. In imagination I had grown from a five-foot nine-inch stripling of 130 pounds to "Big Six" Matty himself, six feet high and 200 pounds.

To my dismay, the coach gave no sign of wanting to win the game. He sent aged and weakened Tarble back to the mound for the last of the eleventh, and as I had foreseen, the Army continued its bombardment. A hit rang out like a sundown salute—and another. Two men on, nobody out.

And now our coach stood up by the bench, his hands on his hips and looked down at the bull pen. One flick of his finger and I would be halfway across to the hill, leaving my humble catcher to anonymity while I went marching up to glory.

After all these years the call was coming—

Then, incredibly, the coach was slowly sitting back down and motioning Tarble to go ahead. My arm hung like lead. Mathewson was gone. Another hit boomed. The game was gone. West Point had won. I crawled up out of the hole and walked slowly to the clubhouse after the scampering players.

That night on the train going home I was thinking about Commencement Day, so soon to come, and about the season, now so soon to be done, when the coach came by to say, "I'd have put you in, but you were tireder'n Tarble. Why, you weren't hardly getting the ball up to the catcher."

Considering how many years that knell to my career had been ringing in my ears, you can understand that it is pretty consoling to learn now how close I came to striking out Eisenhower.

(*Since writing the above, I telegraphed Lieutenant Colonel W. J. Morton, Librarian at the U. S. Military Academy, asking him to wire me just how many hits Eisenhower got off Tarble that day, and have received this reply, "Cadet Eisenhower was not out for the Academy baseball team in 1913."*)

They Are Wrong About Wright

IN his latest book, *When Democracy Builds* (University of Chicago Press), Frank Lloyd Wright, the architect, brings up to date the bucolic yet progressive gospel he has been preaching since 1924 when, in a lecture at Princeton, he began his hosannahs for the ideal dream community, "Broadacre City."

As his evangelistic vision worked on this idyllic new community, his hands began to fashion a scaled model.

His dream took form, and from it many modern city plannings have stemmed, particularly Norman Bel Geddes' "Futurama," which was exhibited at the New York World's Fair to gaping millions. The city should expand into the country. Decentralization demands it.

Now, in *When Democracy Builds*, the renowned architect exhorts eloquently for his Utopian concept, and, if the average reader be not ready for conversion, the book will nevertheless have unquestioned value in that it will dispel the great American myth about Wright himself.

The average American, reading newspapers hurriedly, long ago got it into his head that Wright is some kind of horrendous exotic who flits about building pagan Japanese temples and bestrewing the primrose path with deflowered damsels.

As anyone who knows Wright personally is perfectly aware, nothing could be further from the truth, and, as anyone familiar with American history can now see from

the pages of *When Democracy Builds*, Wright is re-
ligiously, even parochially American in every fiber. He is
Brook Farm come again. He is a latter-day New England
moralist-reformer—in effect, practically a Puritan!

What Wright, his family and apprentices are doing at
the Taliesin Fellowship, near Spring Green, Wisconsin, is
substantially what Theodore Parker, Margaret Fuller,
George Ripley, Nathaniel Hawthorne, and other cosmic
philosophers tried to do in the Brook Farm Experiment
a hundred years ago. Those Transcendentalists tried to
transform the world by setting up an oasis of the simple
life in protest against the crass scramble of industrial slaves
toward the Big City. They believed that man should work
in the soil just enough to gain a livelihood and spend the
rest of his time in high thinking. In Wright's "Broadacre
City," people would live in widely spaced modern homes,
raise their own food, and work in near-by factories.

Brook Farm was the first American communal experiment to owe nothing to any immigrant philosophy, and
Wright's Taliesin Fellowship is belligerently American,
too. The white-maned Master's thunderings in the Wisconsin hills are bellicose blasts against foreign ideologies,
as much as our own centralized greed, against the dead
hand of Great Britain in architecture and finance, against
Europe's "classic" buildings, and he sees little for us in
Russian Communism. He says Americans should exhibit
those marvelous prints of Old Japan as a reproach to the
modern war-hungry, machine-mad Nips, since the prints,
which were the fruit of 300 years of peace, began to die
when the islands went industrial.

Not only does Wright talk as the New England
preachers, from whom he descends in a long line, used to

talk, he writes for the most part in the abstract style of
the Transcendentalists, capitalizing pet gospel words like
Organic Integrity, Usonia, the Good Ground, Integration,
etc., just as they capitalized Insight and the Oversoul. In
occasional pages where his wrath against the Big City, the
rent system, the slums, or the skyscrapers shakes him, he
writes as he draws, simply, directly, boldly, and with
tremendous vitality.

And Wright has what none of the Brook Farmers had,
an impressive authority to back up his words, for he is,
beyond question, the father of modern architecture; he is
more widely accepted and renowned for his actual performances than any other living American artist.

There could be nothing more generically American than
the revivalist fervor with which Wright, in envisioning
Broadacre City's freedom, sanitation, and rural bliss, ex-
coriates the Big City as "an economic Tower of Babel,"
a malign collection of boxes that are "prison cubicles for
the soul of man," a wicked denier of "Jesus's teaching
about the dignity and worth of the individual," a "man-
trap of monstrous dimensions, enormity devouring manhood—anti-Christ today!" He sees the skyscraper as the
devil's own design, robbing man's pocket and maiming
his soul—and he warns against the baleful beauty with
which it glows in the night, "a glimmering verticality, a
gossamer veil, a festive scene-drop hanging there against
the black sky, to dazzle, entertain and amaze."

In his private life, too, Wright is traditionally New
England of the 1840's. Where Henry Thoreau, a kindred
rebel, went to jail because he felt it wrong to pay taxes,
Wright has gone to jail because he felt it wrong to kow-
tow to the conventions about marriage. Both men heard

their consciences demand civil disobedience. And, although Wright long ago went over to the standard orthodoxies for his last and happiest marriage, he still remains to the ignorant a marital ogre, whereas, the simple truth is that he has always been as scornful of surreptitious, covert assignations as were the sternest of the Puritans. A marital cheater has always been too shamefully undignified for Wright to tolerate. When, in the second and third of his four marriages, he did ignore the technical matrimonial conventions, he did so with great personal dignity and candor.

Abstemious of appetite, he has retired regularly at nine-thirty, and when, to be sociable with his guests, he picks up an infrequent highball or cigarette, he does it with the apparent conviction that he'll pay for this in purgatory.

He casts a veritable spell of Puritanic morality upon the young people in his Fellowship, and to be with them, each weekend he'll patiently cross half a continent, so earnest is he about keeping their minds content in Arcady and their souls away from the Big Wicked City.

Heave-ho, Silver!

THE man who has been going around the Loop in a seersucker cutaway and a lawn bow tie, handing out copies of Oscar Hammerstein's *Carmen Jones* is not Bobby Clark, the stage comedian. Neither is he a preacher up from the Ozarks.

He is Ned Alvord, the man who made a fool of the Japanese Government on its own home grounds in 1934.

Mr. Alvord is in town to spread the fame of *Carmen Jones*, the theatrical entertainment at the Erlanger Theater, and to cause its producer, Billy Rose, to be regarded as a Titan of Taste. This is a new role, since Mr. Alvord has, for many years, devoted all his talents to the cause of making the public regard Mr. Rose as the Barnum of Sex.

Mr. Alvord it was who, in the course of press-agenting Mr. Rose's girl show, *Crazy Quilt*, some years back, staged such a public quarrel with Mayor Anderson of Minneapolis over the carnal charms of the show that Mr. Rose's box-office groaned with profits. Mr. Alvord insists that he did not secretly prompt Mayor Anderson to bar *Crazy Quilt* on the grounds that it was too exciting for Minneapolis. But Mr. Alvord's friends have always been skeptical about such a claim of innocence, for this extraordinary press agent's past is dotted with similar plots.

From his youth in Springfield and Joliet and Aurora, Illinois, Mr. Alvord's delight has been to slip into town

ahead of a girl-show and, dressed as a clergyman in lawn
tie and tails, call upon local pastors and persuade them
to denounce the approaching show in the newspapers as
pure Sodom and Gomorrah. A superb actor in his own
right, Mr. Alvord has had little trouble in bringing the
righteous blood of a locality to the boil just in time to
enrich his employers.

Whether Mayor Anderson of Minneapolis was or was
not a victim of this wonderful bit of hocus-pocus, the fact
remains that *Crazy Quilt* did enormous business in neighboring St. Paul, and, in the next mayoralty election, Mr.
Anderson was defeated as a blue-nose "who had made
Minneapolis a hick town in the eyes of the world."

Mr. Alvord performed kindred chores for Mr. Rose's
glamorous *Fort Worth Frontier* in the days when Fort
Worth was out to top the great exposition being held in
neighboring Dallas. He covered virtually every barn from
New Orleans to Kansas City with pagan pictures of Grecian
Europas, clad chiefly in sombreros, riding bulls, and with
lithographs of Parisian nymphs emerging from swamps—
all of whom were to be seen in Mr. Rose's sinful "Casa
Manana" at Fort Worth.

When rural dominies thundered against this art work
on their hen houses, Mr. Alvord obligingly, but tardily,
pasted over the wanton placards new bills advising motor-
ists to drive straight to Fort Worth by route so-and-so and
thus "avoid Dallas bottlenecks."

The inventive Mr. Alvord's chief triumph, however,
came when, in 1934, he arrived in Tokyo ahead of "The
Marcus Show," the first Occidental girl-attraction ever to
play Nippon. Other American and some British girl-shows
had started for Japan, but, says Mr. Alvord, "The maha-

rajahs of India and war lords of Hong Kong and remittance men of Singapore had married so many of the girls
that by the time the company could reach Nippon, it was
nothing but a male minstrel troupe."

This time, however, Mr. Alvord routed the show direct
to Tokyo and, arriving in his tall derby and Prince Albert,
called upon the theater folk and displayed his advertising
matter. For eight hours he sat on his legs urging, through
an interpreter, the twenty-two assembled managers of the
theater to charge $3 for what had been shown in America
for fifty cents.

When the Japanese taboos against stage nakedness were
advanced, Mr. Alvord put on new piety and lectured on
the Yankees' wholesome adoration for the form divine.
Toward evening the white missionary was weak from saki
and dried fish and his feet were asleep, but his evangelistic
spirit rose to new heights when the Japs, after accepting
everything else, absolutely refused to permit "The Spirit
of Silver" number to be shown.

This was a dance performed by Miss Ha Cha San, a
Swede blonde from New Orleans, costumed only in silver
paint, and was the chief flash of the show, although not as
good in Mr. Alvord's eyes as an eccentric dance by an
obscure young man, name of Danny Kaye.

The twenty-two managers told Mr. Alvord that they
had shown his photos of "The Spirit of Silver" to the
Imperial government and had been told, "So sorry."

"All right," bowed Mr. Alvord, "but in humble grati-
tude for the royal hospitality you have given me today, I
must warn you that the Imperial edict will cause your
people to lose face in friendly America."

And when the twenty-two horrified managers squealed,

"How so?" Mr. Alvord took off his glasses and spoke low:

"Our great new President Roosevelt wishes new bonds of friendship with the Orient. A few months ago, to this end, he remonetized silver, that shining metal which flows from you of the East to us of the West, and, in a noble ceremony, which you will, I am sure, now recollect, he had a dream-like statue, 'The Spirit of Silver' placed atop the magnificent State House in Denver, capital of our own silver state, beautiful Colorado.

"And, honorable sirs, it was with the humble thought of complimenting you that America has sent with our little show the very maiden who posed for that statue, Miss Ha Cha San, a living replica of that statue which faces the Pacific from Denver."

There was a hissing of intaken breath in the room, a murmur of excuse pleases. The twenty-two bowed out on tiptoe, and next day the word came that Japan would be honored to see "The Spirit of Silver" twice daily at the American scale of honorable prices.

Mr. Marcus made plenty of money on that trip which, among Mr. Alvord's friends, is called "That time Ned gave Japan the heave-ho, Silver!"

The Great Winnetka Hunt

GEORGE WHARTON, the champion story-teller of Chicago's Loop, was always especially interested in the North Shore, that suburban area in which the socially elect and the Blue Book aspirants make their homes.

George maintained you can stand in the Northwestern depot any day and tell where each woman passenger, as she arrived, had boarded the train. If she wore an evening gown, she came from Evanston; if she wore sports clothes, Lake Forest; a maternity gown, Winnetka.

He said all the males in Lake Forest sniffed at Winnetkans as culture-climbing tradesmen, while Winnetkans said Lake Foresters were nothing but remittance men.

Wharton said that for years Winnetkans made fun of the Onwentsia Club Fox-Hunt, the big event of the Lake Forest social season, describing how the gilded nobles went bouncing and jumping all over Lake County with dogs howling, terrified cows running blind into fences, farmers tearing for their cellars, and sirens screaming, as ambulances rushed to pick unhorsed riders with cracked collarbones out of ditches.

Wharton said he was naturally surprised one day to learn that Winnetka had organized a hunt of its own. He guessed Winnetka simply couldn't stand it any longer to have Lake Forest hog the society columns, so its more social burghers met in the school auditorium and voted, by Robert's Rules of Order, to buy horses, saddles, derbies, and pink coats. They chose a member to go down to Lyon & Healy's, get a horn and take lessons till he learned it. Two members who had recently moved here from New York taught the others how to shout "View Halloo," and they ordered a fox from Sears, Roebuck, but they couldn't find a pack of hounds for sale.

So they put their pride in their pocket and named one of the younger members, whose sister had married into the Lake Forest set, to go ask the Onwentsia Hunt to please lend them their pack for the day. Onwentsia said all right, and on the day when the Winnetka Hunt was all assembled on horseback and waiting at the town hall, up rolled a station wagon and out got one dog—Little Ada was her name. The chauffeur said, sorry but all the other Onwentsia dogs had distemper.

Some riders wanted to call off the Winnetka Hunt, but others said it would make them a laughingstock to back out now, so they put a leash around Little Ada's neck, the Master of the Hounds blew the horn, and the procession clattered out through town toward the Skokie meadows where the fox had already been taken in a hencoop.

Wharton said it was a gay sight, those pink coats against the white picket fences, and everybody at the doorways waving handkerchiefs or copies of the *Yale Review*.

And out from every house, too, came a dog, to fall in behind the procession, for Little Ada had romance in her eye. She'd roll her eyes to the right and then to the left and then her eyelids would droop coquettishly, and by the time the parade hit the Skokie meadows, the Winnetka Hunt had a pack, all right—setters, police dogs, mastiffs, Doberman pinschers, Airedales, bulldogs, terriers, dachshunds—200 at least—with half of them Scotties.

Everybody was happy by now, talking about how good things like this were for the community.

Out into the meadow they came; the Master of the Hounds opened the hencoop door, the fox went like a shadow, Little Ada was unleashed and followed. The pack took out after Little Ada. The horn blew and everybody let off a "View Halloo" that scared some of the horses.

The chase, however, started slowly, for fear the horses would step on the cloud of Pekingese who, at the tail of the pack, were slowed up by the long grass.

But things straightened out pretty soon on that score, for Little Ada, with one eye over her shoulder, got to watching the pack rather than the fox and instead of following Bold Reynard to the north, she went off on a triumphal circle of her own to the south, with the pack yipping at her heels. And no amount of horn-blowing could get her back on the track. The hunt milled, horses bumped, and several matrons fell off. At length eight men on foot caught Little Ada, put the leash on her and everybody trailed home, muttering dark words about those Lake Foresters' sense of humor. Behind came the pack, setters ahead, Pekingese in the rear.

Wharton said the dogs knew they'd never see Little Ada again. It was over. They'd had a pretty good day, at that; and as each dog came to his home gate, he turned in, so that by the time the crestfallen Hunt reached the town hall where the station wagon was waiting, Little Ada hadn't a single admirer in sight.

Reform Is Where You Find It

OTTO MC FEELY, the retired editor and covert reformer of Oak Park, Illinois, is pleased these days at the triumph of another of his many philanthropic crusades. He brought the matter up in discussing, as he so often has, my obtuseness.

"You point out," he said, "how American wars always free some sector of the oppressed, how our early wars extended the Rights of Man, how our Civil War gave theoretical citizenship, at least, to 4,000,000 of our people, how the Spanish-American War freed the Cubans, how World War I doubled the number of our voters. What you fail to see is that this latest war has freed our servant class. They are all out of the kitchen now, serving themselves. I regret that I had no hand in this victory when it came, though I did what I could across many years. For that matter, all I really succeeded in getting done for the Cubans in '98 was to have the lobe of my right ear bitten off in a fight with a fellow rookie in the grandstand at the State Fair Grounds in Indianapolis where the army rendezvoused."

It was later, as a newspaperman in and around Chicago, that he first thought about the servant problem. His only personal experiences had been with hired girls when a small boy in Marion, Indiana, but just from what he could see as a metropolitan adult, the master-class was inconsiderate of domestics. He had seen quite a bit, too, for his talents as a conversationalist had gained him many invitations to homes of the well-to-do.

As a reporter-friend of McFeely, I was once privileged to study his reformer technique. A wealthy friend had asked us out to his palatial home for the weekend. His wife was away on a visit and we would have a season of discussion.

"We'll take a valet with us," said McFeely in phoning the invitation to me, and sure enough on our forty-mile journey into the estated suburbs there rode with us in McFeely's Model T, an ex-preacher, Andrew Polk, a tall, ninety-year-old Virginian who was a janitor when his rheumatism permitted but who lived principally at other times on the hams, $2 bills, overcoats, etc., which McFeely would bring to his basement retreat. Andrew sat in the rear seat with his suitcase, while McFeely and I, pooling our pajamas in one briefcase, sat in front.

Old Andrew, a stately, courtly deacon of a man, liked the ride and spoke to us in a soft, deep voice about pagan trends among the young, about the birds in the wheat and the clouds in the sky. He waited serenely in the back seat, when we arrived at our host's mansion, while McFeely and I entered. For a time we spoke with our host pleasantly, then McFeely asked, "Where shall our man put our things?"

Our host, with darkening brow, snorted, "Your MAN!" To which McFeely replied calmly, "If you're not equipped to put up valets, we'll come again some other time—just to lunch."

Our host went to the window and stared incredulously at Andrew, who was leaning back admiring the estate. Trapped, our host eventually blurted, "Oh, bring him in," and McFeely and I rose, and went out to the car. While McFeely gave the rheumatic old man his arm going up the walk, I came behind with Andrew's suitcase. Just before we reached the door I heard McFeely whisper, "Andrew, speaking of prayer, our host inside here was once a devout churchman but is now the champion back-slider of Lake County."

Old Andrew nodded gravely and when we entered the door, bowed with great dignity to our host, then stood looking at him as King David undoubtedly looked at Absalom. Our host hemmed and hawed, unable to decide whether to tell a valet where the servant quarters were or to ask a deacon to sit down. Eventually McFeely and I took Andrew to a room where an easy chair by a window overlooked beautiful fields. McFeely brought the radio over to him while I got him a pitcher of water and a glass. "Enjoy yourself, now, till dinner, Andrew," said Mc-Feely. "Do you mind standing behind us tonight and serving us—just us?"

"Anything to repay you for this weekend," said the old man.

That night Andrew did very well at dinner, consider-ing his rheumatism, for McFeely and I had rustled up one of our host's canes for him, and we only heard him drop three dishes in the near-by kitchen as he came and went with our food. At each crash, McFeely and I would launch more loudly into anecdotes, while our host sat in pained politeness, eating but little of what the maid brought him.

After dinner we told Andrew he needn't help with the dishes; we had put out for his use a chair and a sprayer full of Flit on the lawn beside some white flowers which would open in the moonlight.

The rest of us went to bed early, our host pleading indigestion, and McFeely and I knew nothing more till around six o'clock next morning when the door of our room burst open and in stormed our host, his long nightshirt slapping his shins.

"Now, you've gone too far," he bellowed, as he stood between the twin beds glaring at us. "I was sound asleep when I felt somebody in the room and looked, and there was this goddam valet of yours sitting in a chair beside the bed looking at me—just looking at me! I sat up and he said, 'Son, join me in praying for your redemption'— and I—"

McFeely rose haughtily, held up a palm toward our host, and said, "We must be going. One of the truest gentlemen in the world has been misunderstood." I arose, too. Our host stamped out. We dressed and went out into the yard where old Andrew stood with three dogs and one cat playing around his feet and the birds singing on branches so close that they seemed to be actually on his shoulders.

"Andrew," said McFeely, helping the old man into the Ford, "we're starting on an all-day drive. Think where you'd like to go."

To me, McFeely said, "You crank the car, I've got to go back and get Andrew's bag."

A Founding Father Returns

IN the U. S. Senate building on November 23, 1945, assorted senators and congressmen were inquiring into the reasons for the disaster at Pearl Harbor. Some 300 people were packed in closely arrayed chairs, under the movie camera shelves, around the walls, in behind the map easels, and back of the august Inquisitors. In what was practically the middle of the room, facing the committee and flanked on either side by tablesful of lawyers, reporters, and stenographers, was an empty chair, wherein on previous days had sat admirals and Army officers telling what they knew and trying to hold onto their stories in the face of badgering questions.

It was the hot seat and the word had gone around that it would be hotter than ever today, for Cordell Hull, the man some of the Inquisitors were really after, was to testify.

The spectators' seats and standing spots had filled early, and now the police were busy at the door. From the marble corridors outside came the murmuring of many disappointed citizens.

Finally, there was a special rustle at the door and an exhalation in the craning crowd. A white head suddenly towered above the audience, the movie lights flared on, and Cordell Hull, all in black, his overcoat draped over his shoulders, his handsome face, pale from long illness, his hair dazzling in the spotlight, came to the witness chair.

He poised his six feet three inches like an ancient white sycamore, lean, weathered, frail, but still standing after many storms, and ready, now, for a new one. You could half-hear, half-feel a gasp of admiration running through the crowd, for the old statesman with the spotlight on his long face, was as classic as a Greek statue. Indeed, he might have been coming to sit as a model for a class in antique art—a Roman senator facing judgment.

A woman next to me leaned forward and whispered to herself, "Beautiful! Beautiful!" as if she had suddenly been shown an ermine coat.

Cordell Hull is one of the few men whom old age has made handsomer—whom decay has made nobler and statelier.

Standing there, he had more presence than anyone I have ever seen since the days of Christy Mathewson, the baseball pitcher, or Albert J. Beveridge, the orator. And, as I remember them, his presence was greater than theirs, for his was wholly without self-consciousness.

Hull had risen from the sickroom where he had lain since his resignation as Secretary of State. He had insisted that his physician let him testify as to whether he had or had not provoked the Japanese into making their surprise attack upon Pearl Harbor. His physician had said he could appear for forty-five minutes—no longer. And as he stood there this seemed too much.

The extraordinary thing was that he had actually been gone from the very center of the world for only a few months. Only out of the secretary's chair for a little while, yet here he was stalking back to us as if from Bunker Hill.

As he stood there, he might have been George Washington or Thomas Jefferson. He looked like a Founding Father. On that white and serene old face was the story of the Republic, a particular blend of idealism and backwoods cunning—the aquiline nose of Uncle Sam himself, the wide, mobile mouth of the frontiersman, the heavy eyelid of the dreamer half hiding the steady eye which could look through a foreign aristocrat or drop a squirrel at 200 paces—either one.

It wasn't the composure of Lincoln nor the gravity of Robert E. Lee that you thought of, as he stood there. No, it was something further back than that, something back of even Old Hickory Jackson. Hull seemed to come out of the Revolution itself, a place neither North nor South, a time when the Republic was taking root. The terms Democrat or Republican, New Dealer, Old Dealer— none of them fit him now. You couldn't say he was a Tennessean, though he had been reared there. You couldn't remember that he had once been a poor mountain boy, or a shrewd, sagacious senator. You could hardly think of him now as our most famous Secretary of State, so wholly had he, in his retirement, passed on into the American Olympus.

And his foes on the committee, the ones who had hoped to wring from him the confession that he and President Roosevelt had enticed the Japs into giving them the war they wanted, these Inquisitors knew the jig was up before ever the old man spoke a word. Such questions as were put to him were put almost with reverence, and no one grew sharp or prying with him even after he warmed to his task and lost the frailty of voice that had been his at the beginning of his testimony.

When told that his forty-five minutes were up and that the committee wished not to detain him longer, he said to go ahead, he was all right. And he held the committee for fifteen minutes more, damning the Japs with solemn unemotional pronouncements and sage ruralism, describing the devices, the patient arguments, the long beseechments he had employed to keep the mad little yellow men from the course which was to end them among the atomic cinders.

At length, for his own health's sake, Hull's testimony was courteously ended by the committee chairman, and, bowing his thanks, he walked his stately walk out through the crowd which stood, and for the first time during the inquiry, broke into rolling applause.

Behind him stood the witness chair which had for him turned out to be no hot seat at all, but instead something more like a cracker box—or a throne.

The Big Shoulders Sag

THE shoulders of the City of Big Shoulders aren't so big any more.

And the sundowns don't glow out beyond the canyons of the Loop with that red prairie-fire smolder they used to have.

Carl Sandburg has quit the city whose greatest poet and interpreter he so long has been. Quit it, thirty years to the springtime, after his bomb of a book, *Chicago Poems,* went off with a detonation that rocketed him from obscurity to a surprised seat beside Whitman on the American literary Olympus.

No poem, except Whitman's "When Lilacs Last in the Dooryard Bloom'd" ever did to me what Sandburg's "Chicago" did in that spring of 1916 when Henry Holt and Company published his first book, *Chicago Poems.* Six months before, I had passed through Chicago for the first time, been fascinated by the place, and had come back to wangle a job on the *Herald,* a newspaper which Chicago's most fabulous editor, James Keeley, had started. Coming to the city from the aged and sentimental quietude of Philadelphia, and still a sophomore in spirit, I hadn't yet been able, after half a year in Chicago, to tell anybody why I was so inwardly rhapsodic about the new town.

But before I had finished the first of "Chicago's" two pages of free verse I knew. In fact I remember exactly where, in the poem, I knew. It was at that line where Sandburg, after admitting all that the world said about Chicago's brutality, its gunmen, its fleshpots, defiantly sings—

. . . So I turn once more to those who sneer at this my city,
     and I give them back the sneer and say to them:
Come and show me another city with lifted head and singing
     so proud to be alive and coarse and cunning.

Here was "a tall bold slugger set vivid against the little soft cities. . . ."

> Hog Butcher for the World. . . .
> Stormy, husky, brawling,
> City of the Big Shoulders. . . .

This was what I had been wanting to say and couldn't. This was the reckless, titanic city itself. Yet, over the violence every so often, as the pages turned, would come drifting the smoke of quiet pity, the veiling romance of yellow dust on bumblebees' wings, the healing dusk over drab shanties, the mist over sea-blown lake fronts, the shadows over prostitutes in the low-lit streets—mist, dust, smoke and shadow. On one page swaggering icemen would roar up backstairs, on another, girls in dreams would feel "a waver of love, tender as dew, impetuous as rain."

Here Sandburg would sketch the grim epic life of a skyscraper, but turn the pillar into a brother of smoke and stars before his poem was done. Here an expectant mother would brood among red poppies, and there the "bunkshooter" Billy Sunday would be skinned alive by a berserk Sandburg who had seen the evangelist haranguing on the lake-front.

Sandburg had revealed the fierce, bragging Nation's

Freight Handler of a city to me, and from that day I have never wanted to live anywhere else.

The next morning after I read *Chicago Poems*, I began urging the *Herald's* feature editor to hire Sandburg to write a Thanksgiving poem for us. It was tough, for Sandburg's poetry didn't rhyme, and besides, I was told, he was just a $27.50-a-week reporter on a radical tabloid in town, *The Day Book*. But I bulled it through, and for $25 he wrote the poem called "Fire Dreams," reprinted later in *Cornhuskers*, Sandburg's second book of poems.

From that time on there has been only one moment of rift in what is now thirty years of friendship. That came in 1924 when, in Righeimer's tavern one night, each discovered that the other was writing about Abraham Lincoln. For a few minutes we stalked around each other like strange tomcats, then I found he only wanted Lincoln alive, and he found I only wanted Lincoln dead. So we martyred the Great Emancipator again, cut him up, divided him, and traded material ever after, he giving, however, far more than he received.

Launched on his career as a platform artist, he has had a wide range indeed. H. L. Mencken once said that of all living American literary men, Sandburg had the best chance for immortality. "He's taken three cuts at it," said Mencken. "His poetry may well be the best poetry, his biography of Lincoln may be the best biography, and his *Rootabaga Stories* may be the fairy tales of the future. One of the three should hit and maybe all three."

So long as Sandburg lived, as he did in past decades, in the near-by Michigan sand-dunes, Chicago could still claim him, but now that he has moved to Flat Rock,

North Carolina, on the edge of the Blue Ridge, the cord is really snapped.

What took him away was his family's need for an easier climate, his daughter Helga's wish for a larger farm and horses to ride, and his prize-winning billy goats' need for a hilly country. He told his family to pick out the place they wanted, anywhere, and he'd buy it.

That country, North Carolina and Virginia, has now wooed the three men who in the 1910s and '20s made Chicago the literary capital of America as Mencken called it. Edgar Lee Masters lives in Virginia, Sherwood Anderson had his home there when he died—and now Sandburg, the great old Swede, has settled close by.

Were any of the three ever truly at home in Chicago? They did their greatest work here, sure enough, but there keeps coming back to me disquietingly Synge's one-line explanation of why his imaginative playboy was not at home in the Western World, "He was a poet in a merchant's town."

Orchids to Mrs. Einstein

AS I get the story, Professor Einstein and his wife, when they moved from Europe to the United States, made their entry by the West Coast where they were feted, wined, dined, and luncheoned in the best California manner before they made their way by acclamatory stages to Manhattan.

Among the first of the Eastern functions which honored the great mathematician was a luncheon given by the *New York Times,* with that newspaper's intellectual counselor and professional greeter, Dr. John H. Finley, acting as host. A distinguished scholar in his own right, Dr. Finley had no trouble in assembling twenty to thirty of the city's top male publishers, scholars, and scientists to meet the professor.

Elated by the brilliance of the gathering, Dr. Finley on the day of the affair was staggered somewhat by the arrival of Mrs. Einstein with her husband. There had been some mistake in the invitation, and the lady had thought herself included. All rallied handsomely to make the lady comfortable among so many men. She was charming, cultured, gracious, and full of social aplomb as became fully apparent when, getting a spot of ink on her nose when she signed the guest book, she laughed gaily about her near-sightedness.

There was quite a space of time for the company to mill around her and her husband, for Dr. Finley delayed luncheon until he could get the seating arrangements adjusted and an orchid corsage brought in for her. Some of the guests, however, were typical New York executives who, big with appointments for the afternoon, began to grow restive at the delay. Dr. Finley eventually had to quit waiting for the orchids and sit everybody down at the table.

The conversation was scintillating, and Dr. Finley had all but forgotten the missing bouquet when a waiter stole in on cat's feet and deftly slid a plate bearing the corsage in at Mrs. Einstein's left hand. Dr. Finley sighed and shut his eyes in relief, but when he opened them, they proceeded to pop right out of his head, for Mrs. Einstein was eating the orchids!

She was forking them down with daintiness but relish the while she listened to her husband talk of Time and Space and Things to Come.

Dr. Finley's heart stood still. Were orchids poison? Didn't they grow in tropical shadows like the deadly nightshade? He looked frantically around the table. What luck to have present, at this crisis, the cream of the nation's scientists!

Excusing himself, he retired to the anteroom and sent back a waiter to tell the best physician at the table that he was wanted on the telephone. The medico listened to Dr. Finley's anxious whispers, but could do nothing. He had never heard of anyone eating an orchid. Neither had any of the chemists, bacteriologists, stomach specialists, engineers, or publishers of encyclopedias, who, one by one, were brought out for pumping, while Dr. Finley painfully peeped through the crack in the door to be sure Mrs. Einstein was still up.

The luncheon was almost over when Dr. Finley finally got his answer. It was from the head of a botanical garden in Boston who, over long distance, said that while the thing was unprecedented he couldn't see any harm in it. By this time Dr. Finley felt that his long absence from the head of the table and the flitting about of so many guests demanded an explanation, so he confessed the whole business to Mrs. Einstein who laughed like the lady she is and said she had thought the orchids "just another of those California salads."

Woollcott, Horner & White

WITH William Allen White's autobiography on the stands and his letters to be published by the University of Chicago as edited by Professor Walter Johnson, who is also writing White's life, I miss the "Sage of Emporia" more than ever.

Not that I ever knew him intimately, unless it be that anyone who met him knew him intimately right off. The round-faced little editor from Kansas had that same quality that Ruth Gordon, the actress, described when she spoke at the memorial services to Alexander Woollcott. Miss Gordon came quietly but bravely to the speaker's platform in that sad ceremony and began, "I was Alexander Woollcott's best friend."

She waited, swallowing hard, and as she did so, every one of the 450 friends of Woollcott assembled there, squirmed at her effrontery. Then she went on, "And so was each of you."

And in the sigh of affection that went up to her from each of the 450 was the realization that she had spoken the exact truth. Both White and Woollcott had that gift of making new friends feel like old friends, tried and proven.

I never saw William Allen White, I suppose, more than a dozen times across twenty years, yet each time, he would make it seem as if we met daily. He would work that magic with thousands.

There was the time I saw him and his wife motor into Topeka from their Emporia home, the two of them riding on the front seat with their houseman, chauffeur, and friend while the back seat remained empty. The car, the chauffeur, Mr. and Mrs. White had all grown old together, and enjoyed each other, you could see that.

Later on White and his wife were so pleased because when they got the flu they got it at the same time in New York and could go to the hospital together and have both beds in one room.

There was the time when he went to Springfield, Illinois, to the dedication of the new post office at New Salem, where Lincoln had once put letters in hickory pigeonholes. White was disappointed at the absence of Governor Henry Horner, who more than any other one man had made that reconstructed village the marvel that it is. The governor's doctors had, at the last minute, refused to allow him to attend this service that was the one thing in all the world he wanted most to see.

While the ceremonies were on, White suddenly leaned across and whispered that he'd like to go back to town early so he could call on the sick governor and tell him what a success the day was. We eased out and went back to the governor's mansion, where White sat for a time beside the sickbed and talked, the tears running down Horner's face. White thought he ought to be going, that he was putting a strain on the invalid, but Horner wouldn't have it, and put White at ease by telling him a story about himself and President Roosevelt, knowing how White collected anecdotes of the Presidents. (White's books on Wilson and Coolidge still carry more reality in them than anything else written about either man.)

"When I was a boy," said Horner, "my grandfather told me that if I was to be invited to nice places, I mustn't crumple crackers in soup. So I didn't, but I never had soup without wanting to—bad.

"Then came a time in 1933 when President Roosevelt had six midwestern governors to lunch, and there was the soup—and there were the crackers and me eating them one at a time as my grandfather would have wished. I was talking to someone at my left when from my right where the President sat there came a sound that froze me —the sound of crumpling crackers, crumpling and splashing lightly in soup. I turned my head slowly, incredulously and from the corner of my eye saw the President of the United States, scion of the bluest blood in America, crackling crackers into his soup with aristocratic assurance.

"I dropped whatever conversation I was making, seized my crackers with both hands, snowed them into my soup and damned my dear grandfather for fifty wasted years."

White said, as he went away soon after, that Horner was his kind of an American, which Horner certainly was, for both of them were fighters, humorists, shrewd politicians, White a Republican and Horner a Democrat, but each so independent and so intelligent about good government as to be brothers under the skin.

And there was the time White, coming back from New York, told me about the dinner he'd just attended—a dinner given in the depths of the depression by a powerful railroad magnate who had been to Europe to study conditions and had come home to explain to important people what the United States must do to recover prosperity.

"The mogul got up," said White, "and said the American farmer must meet his competition. He said he'd seen how the European farmer prospered by having no nonsense about his children going to college, or owning radios or automobiles. He said the farmer over there made one Sunday suit last a lifetime, then the son wore it his lifetime, too. He said the farmers there saved every little bit of manure, piled it against the house, kept warm by it in winter, and used it on the fields in the spring."

At this point, the magnate asked White as representative of rural America, what he thought. White answered: "What you say may be true. Maybe the American farmer will have to come down to the level you advocate, but I want to tell you that the day before he does it, he's going to go down to the depot and take your railroad all apart."

Life with Uncle Eggs

THE three little girls, away up on the third floor of the mansion, slept lightly for they never knew when a low whistle would wind up the staircase and a musical male voice would whisper, "Any young ladies up there like a lobster supper with a gentleman?"

They would whisper, "Yes," tiptoe back to their rooms, get dressed, and then slide noiselessly down the banister so as not to awaken their aunt on the second floor. In the big dining room their Uncle "Eggs" would be setting out lobster salad and certain crisp rolls which he said he could get nowhere but at Rector's this late at night after the Follies was over.

They would eat and talk till two, three o'clock, hushing each other when the girls giggled too loud, for their Uncle "Eggs" was a very funny man and could make anybody laugh when he wanted.

Yes, he was a very funny man, indeed.

He was Bert Williams, the finest musical comedy artist I have seen in thirty years of theater-going. Funny as could be and sad, too, yet he never was as sad as he could have been had his great dramatic ability been given free rein. Always he impersonated lugubrious Negro rustics or porters or preachers on the stage, whereas in private life he was a well-read and affluent gentleman, so proud of his British birth that he never became an American citizen. His three nieces and the people in the Ziegfeld

Follies where he starred so long called him "Eggs" because his first name was Egbert—Egbert Austin Williams, a name that became him as a Bahama-born grandson of a Danish fruit-grower.

When he sang to the three nieces that he had brought to his New York home in 1913 when their mother, his wife's sister, died in Chicago, it was in a light, sweet baritone, a voice theater audiences never heard. And when the little nieces would ask him why he didn't sing this beautiful way on the stage instead of just croaking away down, he'd answer, "Now, you don't think I'd lose my trade mark just because some sentimental women asked me to?"

One of these nieces, Mrs. Charlotte Tyler, was telling these things about him the other day while she did her work cataloguing songs at the Newberry Library. She said he'd sing to his nieces by the hour, sitting crossways of the grand piano stool in the music room of the big house he had at 2309 Seventh Avenue, New York. He'd be working out melodies for some of the songs which made him one of the highest salaried and best-loved stars of the American stage—songs like "Nobody," "Jonah Man," and "When the Moon Shines on the Moonshine So Merrily." Only occasionally did he write the words; he had collaborators for that, but the music, the almost unheard shadows of melody which stole along behind the sepulchral bass with which he talked off his songs—the music was what he worked on.

And many a time the three nieces would half awaken late at night and hear him at the piano, all alone downstairs there fingering tunes till dawn, and they'd slip back into sleep feeling very warm and safe and wonderful.

"Life with Uncle 'Eggs' was wonderful all the time," Mrs. Tyler remembers. "It was like living with Santa Claus. He never raised his voice; he was never angry. Always there were presents, but sometime during the day he'd sit down with us in his library—he had a big library with lots of fine bindings—and he'd read to us—serious books, things he thought would be good for us. We had to be good in school to please him. He always carried a book in his pocket; I remember him wearing out a copy of *The Rubáiyát*."

Bert Williams had got good grades in grammar and high school himself, in Los Angeles where he grew up. Mrs. Tyler has his report card in the seventh grade with everything marked "Excellent." He had had a happy boyhood, she recalls, and wanted his orphaned nieces to be happy, too.

"He would tell us about his father," she says, "Frederick Williams, son of a Danish orange grower of the West Indies, and Sarah Moncur of mixed Danish, French, and Negro blood." Frederick was, as Mrs. Tyler heard, "a fair man with red hair and Buffalo Bill mustaches who got mad when his boy Bert quit high school at sixteen to get a job barking with a medicine show."

Trailing his boy he found him; hid behind a tree, listening to the long-legged, long-armed kid "spiel" from a platform, then edged up and told him to come home. But the boy, even then a mesmerizing talker, gave his father such a story about the show inside that the parent smoothed down his red hair, went in—and was lost. His boy had sung well in the Episcopalian choir, but he never knew he was funny, too. So Father Williams told his boy to go ahead.

This must have been in 1892, for Williams had several seasons of minstrel work before joining George Walker, the cake-walking, resplendent dude, in 1895—a partnership which carried them in their all-colored extravaganza, "In Dahomey," all over America and to London where as the climax of an eight months' run they appeared by command at Buckingham Palace, as Mrs. Tyler remembers, "for the birthday party of the Prince of Wales, who's now married to Mrs. Windsor."

"In Dahomey" and "Bandanna Land" made both Williams and Walker rich men, and after Walker died in 1909, Williams went into vaudeville at $2,000 a week till Florenz Ziegfeld starred him in the Follies at $62,400 a year no matter how long or short the show ran. "This," says Mrs. Tyler, "lasted twelve years with no signed contract between them—just their word."

The great house which Uncle "Eggs" gave his wife for a birthday present was almost too elegant for him, well-dressed and always be-caned man though he was.

"My aunt wouldn't let him smoke in the house—too many ashes—" says Mrs. Tyler, "and she wouldn't let him have a dog."

Once, she recalls, he did bring home a toy bulldog, "Snowball," anyway, and when he'd come in for dinner, "he'd pick up the little thing and ask it, 'Did they mistreat you today?' and Snowball would whine back at him. He'd keep right on, 'Did they lock you up in the cellar?' and the dog would lift its face to him and whine, and 'Did they starve you?' and it would answer.

"One day when they were going through their routine, my aunt broke out, 'That dog's a damn liar!'"

"As a boy in California," says Mrs. Tyler, "he had to

learn the art of make-up when he went off with minstrel shows, for he was really fair, with soft, gently waving hair and looked like a Frenchman. His blood was French, Negro, and Danish—more Danish than anything. He got to be expert at 'blacking up' but said it was harder than it looked. I know he'd tell about how hard it was to get just the right make-up on Eddie Cantor, when Eddie was a young singer in the Follies and decided to go in for burnt-cork."

Bert Williams, according to Mrs. Tyler, wasn't much for talking to women other than his wife, his three nieces, whom he reared, and a group of middle-aged women who called themselves "The Follies Mothers' Club."

"That was a group of women who had daughters in Ziegfeld's Follies and who sort of banded together to protect their daughters from the 'stage-door Johnnies,' " says Mrs. Tyler. "Now they'd be called 'wolves.' It was about this that the mothers would talk to my uncle. They thought Bert Williams, as star of the show, and kindly as he was, was somebody they could be confidential with. They thought he'd have ways of getting a line on the stage-door Johnnies, since the stagehands, doormen, actors, managers, and box-office boys were confidential with him, and he'd get all the facts and tell them straight.

"They'd sit and talk to him and he'd advise them. They called him 'Eggs' as people who were close to him always did.

"But outside of those mothers and his own family, he was a man's man. My, how he liked to talk to men. He'd stand, leaning on his cane, at 135th and Lexington Avenue in New York, not far from his home, talking to friends. He'd say that all he ever knew about the Southern Negro, whom he played on the stage, he picked up just listening at 135th and Lexington. Born in the Bahamas and raised in Los Angeles, he'd never seen those Deep South preachers or plug-hat poker players he impersonated."

Considering how perfect was Williams' pantomime in his famous solo "poker game," it is surprising to learn that he didn't like cards, but got his material from watching other men lose. Mrs. Tyler feels sure her uncle got his equally famous ghost cat story, "We Can't Do Nothin' Till Martin Comes" (a great stage and phonograph favorite of the 1920s), from listening to superstitious folk-talk on his favorite street corner.

Wealthy from his young manhood when in the middle 1890s he and George Walker struck it rich with their all-colored musical comedies, Williams had to acquire by observation the comic actions and inflections of the Negro who did servile tasks and who shuffled lazily away from toil—that stock low-comedy stage character which was in its time as standardized as the little be-derbied Jew peddler and the spluttering Dutch butcher and the belligerent Irish "Mick," and the broken-tongued, banana-selling "Dago."

"My uncle was very fond of George Walker," Mrs. Tyler says, "although George bought diamonds all the time while Uncle 'Eggs' bought one a year for his wife. I've heard him tell how funny George was and how as a boy in Topeka, Kansas, George told his grandmother, who raised him, how bright he was in school—got 100 in everything except arithmetic and in that he got 600! The grandmother, good ignorant old soul, told it all over Topeka."

An Episcopalian all his life, Bert Williams was always

attracted by the Jewish faith. Mrs. Tyler says, "He learned to read and speak Yiddish. He'd go to synagogues sometimes and come home and discuss with us what the rabbi had said or how the singing had sounded.

"He liked sociability, joined the Masons at Edinburgh, Scotland, became a thirty-third-degree member and was buried by them when he died. He belonged to two regiments of the National Guard, the 8th in Illinois and the 15th in New York—honorary captain in each.

"Once he told his wife and us three nieces to sit in the reviewing stand on Fifth Avenue in New York to see him ride in a military parade. He told us to look for him right behind his close friend, Colonel William Hayward. He had on his uniform and boots, all dressed up. And we waited, all ready to scream when he'd come past, but he never came. There was the 15th and Colonel Hayward but no Uncle 'Eggs,' and that evening we asked where he'd been and he said, 'On the way down, my horse just turned out of the parade and went down in a subway entrance. I talked to it when it left the parade and I talked to it down there in the subway, but I never did find out why it wanted to go there or why it didn't want to come out.' "

Mrs. Tyler's first memory of Bert Williams is that of his coming to her mother's house at 55th and Cottage Grove in Chicago to court her aunt, Charlotte Johnson:

"After they were married in 1897, he'd give us girls $10 in gold for every cake or every plate of biscuits we'd bake him, and he'd give us $100 apiece in gold at Christmas, but this first time he came courting, he had on high brown patent leather shoes that hurt him awful. We talked him into taking them off and when he started home he couldn't get him on, so he walked off in his socks, his shoes in one hand and his cane in the other, and went up the Elevated steps and gave the shoes to a man who said they'd fit him; and then he rode on down to the Loop and walked over to the Sherman Hotel, where he stayed, and went right in through the lobby in his socks.

"The next evening he told it so funny, we little girls laughed for three days and nights."

Backwoods Aristocrat

FOR two weeks now, I've been unable to get far into Isabel McKinney's *Mr. Lord*, the biography of Dr. Livingston C. Lord, whose presidency of the Eastern Illinois State Teachers College at Charleston had so inspiring an influence on so many neighboring farm boys.

What interrupts are memories of a neighbor and patron of Dr. Lord's Normal, a remarkable pioneer named Martin Tarble at whose farm away back in the hills I spent a memorable weekend in the early 1920s.

The old man's hand was waving in a gesture both quaint and regal as I approached. He was standing in front of his long, low, gray farmhouse and many paintless farm buildings. Later he told me paint salesmen were swindlers, befuddling farmers with fancy talk. He stood tall, dignified, his feet bare, his overalls spotless and blue, his mustache as long and pointed as Napoleon III's, and his nose bold and his eye sharp with humor. He made me think of one of those rustic Balkan princes, half peasant, half aristocrat—a type the prairies see no more.

Nodding toward the horizon of his wide acres, he said, "Looks pretty but ain't. Land's poor. My parents settled north of here on the rich prairie, but the horse flies bit 'em and they retreated down onto this timber and high clay ground. You hear about this as Lincoln's country. Never knew the man myself. Come on in the house."

In the airy, very comfortable, very clean parlor he

seated himself at an ancient reed organ and said, "Bought this off Sears, Roebuck in 1895; never had played any instrument but thought I could enjoy myself with an organ. You're in the theater business and I want you to settle something for me; tell me if what I do on it is music—tell me and tell me true."

Then he put his fingers in the deeply grooved ivory keys, placed his bare feet on the worn pedals. I remember the sun, the breeze and the call of a rain crow coming in at the open door.

From the organ came dissonance like Debussy's, perhaps, strange callings and sighings, rushing exultations with now and then a hint, rather than a bar of "The Star-Spangled Banner," but on old Mr. Tarble's face was harmony.

He stopped. "Is it music?" he demanded of me, and when I stammered that, if he'd visit me in Chicago, I'd get him to experts who'd tell for sure, he dismissed it all with a smile. "Thanks! Now I want to show you some old pictures." He brought in a small trunk and began taking out daguerreotypes and giving biographies of the sitters— sketches that could have gone into another *Spoon River Anthology*. He lingered longest over the girls, dark, fresh-faced girls of the '70s.

"This one," he mused, "how she did want to get married! I used to go horseback fourteen miles after work to spend a couple of hours callin' on her. Get home about sunup. When her parents would go to bed, we'd turn chairs. You know what that is? Well, you take two kitchen chairs, put 'em side by side, facing opposite, and sit there and hug and kiss."

As he kept dipping into the portraits, an infant grandchild crawled into the room, and toppled into the trunk. With his foot the old man deftly flipped the baby out, while his hands opened the clasps of a velvet-lined daguerreotype case.

"I declare," he muttered, "there's my little old first wife." He shut the case gently and opened another. "Here's a man used to buy my hogs." He sprang to his feet and brought from a closet a stovepipe hat. "I used to wear this when we hauled fat hogs to town. Get ten or twelve neighbors to come with their wagons and we'd have a parade, me and the hat in the front wagon; parade all over town. You could get all the help in the world that way."

Next from the trunk came a sheaf of newspaper clippings which, with a snort of depreciation, he tried to put aside, but I read them. They were shrewd, homely satires on neighborhood Progress and the Machine Age he had written for local newspapers. One, I remember, counseled farmers not to oppose the oil-well invasion since, while it ruined their streams and land, it would assure them new, cheap kindling for their fireplaces—oil-soaked fish.

Another daguerreotype prompted him to point to his eldest son and say, "Looks like Charles, there. When Charles graduated from the Normal he wanted to go to the university and study agriculture. 'Hell,' I told him, 'you can learn more from your own father; he's worn out three farms himself.'" (Incidentally, Charles today is the best-known county farm agent in Illinois.) "I wasn't brought up much on education myself" (I had noted newspapers and magazines piled beside his chair at the fireplace), "but when my children wanted to go to the Normal and be taught by this famous Dr. Lord, I said,

'All right, I'll have the lumber sawed and you boys—
there was four of 'em wanting to go—haul it to Charleston
and build a house and furnish it out of the extra furniture
here at home, and your sister will cook for you and go to
the Normal, too. You'll not be running home, wasting
time. If you are going to the Normal, I want you to
really go.'

"They took me up on it; built the house, lived right
there and did all right, too, in the Normal. Went through
and most of 'em went on to one college or another."

He broke off as if suspecting that he sounded boastful.
He spun his mustachios searching for something self-
deprecatory to say, ripe, seasoned intelligence playing
across his face.

"I'd like to come up to Chicago and have them that
know, tell about the organ-playing, but I never liked
cities. Only place I ever liked outside of here was Hot
Springs. I've had a winter place there for a long time.
Went there first because I'd had the lung fever one
winter and couldn't wait for spring. Told the folks I'd be
gone for a spell, stuck a couple of hundred dollars in my
pocket, walked across the country and caught a train for
Hot Springs because it sounded good. I always thought
the railroads didn't pay their share of taxes and bore
heavily on the farmers, so I picked up a slate and pencil
as I started out and when the conductors came through
I'd write 'I'm deaf and dumb and must get to Arkansaw.'

"Got there without paying a cent; meals, too. Just
wanted to see if it could be done."

He stroked his mustachios which were now fully as
pointed as the glints of amusement in his baronial blue
eyes.

"Send Off, and Get
Lots of Mail"

FOR the past ten years, Chicago's drama critics have missed the helpful criticisms that used to be visited upon the profession by George Wharton, a political payroller around town, who as an ex-newspaperman, ex-theater manager, and persistent student of drama and literature, was well equipped for his ministrations to the reviewers.

A popular and privileged character in the Loop for some thirty years, Wharton knew all journalists and theatrical personages and would regale them with the weaknesses, idiosyncrasies, and inhibitions of the drama critics. When a new play opened, George would read the reviews, then attend the drama, and come around to the critics' offices, explaining how many errors they had made.

The only reason the critics didn't kill him was that they loved him, a huge, fat man with a poker face whose deep humor and withering ridicule was illumined by the most fantastic imagination. For example, he would go around town saying, just as if it were true, that the entire corps of drama critics wore second-hand clothes given them by those theatrical stars whom they had praised effusively. Each critic, he declared, had an actor upon whom he could depend for raiment. Ashton Stevens' reputation as a sartorial dandy, said George, had been entirely built on the cast-off finery of William Faversham; Charles Collins always wore the discarded suits of Walter Hampden; Amy Leslie had been appareled from 1890 to 1910 by what Lillian Russell had no longer desired and from 1910 to 1915 by Trixie Friganza and from 1915 to 1930 by Sophie Tucker; and I wore the abandoned costumes of Alfred Lunt, let out at the seams.

None of us drama critics were possessed of enough wit nor capacity in practical joking to get back at Wharton. It took a sports editor, Howard Mann, to do that.

Wharton told Mann one day about his new job, the secretaryship of the Buy-Illinois-Products Commission, which obliged him to sit most of the day in a barren office on the top floor of the old Board of Trade Building, one flight above the highest elevator, waiting vainly for the telephone to ring or the door to open.

"Even the mailman never comes," lamented George, which prompted Mann to buy some dozens of magazines, clip all the advertising coupons, and send each to the advertiser with George Wharton's name typewritten thereon. It was the work of days and expensive, too, what with the cost of mailing and the enclosing of dimes and quarters for samples.

Having done his deed of mercy, Mann sat back and waited. Three days later George, who was about sixty, hove his great bulk into Mann's office, sat down, glared at Mann for a time, then said, "You - - - -! I don't get any mail, eh? Well, I walked up that last flight of stairs to my office this morning about ten o'clock and stopped! I thought snow had drifted against my door. Looking closer, I found it was mail: catalogues, letters, first, second, third, fourth class. I had to call for the janitor to hold me while I leaned over to unlock the door. I've spent all day sorting the stuff.

"The afternoon delivery was twice as big, and I can't yet find out one tenth of what I seem to have written for. Just from what I can get at a glance, I have asked how to start correspondence courses in physical culture, ventriloquism, civil service, cartooning, hotel management, life insurance, polite conversation, electric welding, the detection of criminals, short-story writing, table manners, and the feeding and care of stud horses.

"I must hurry home now, get to bed early so I can beat the mailman down in the morning, else he will pile it up and break down my door, which is state property. Good-bye and go to hell!"

Next evening he was back, to revile Mann with comments on his infantile sense of humor, and to read off with some pleasure the advertisers who had responded to his coupons.

"It appears," said he, "that I have inquired for immediate information, at no obligation to myself, on vacations in Hawaii, on how to become my own boss through the operation of a steam vulcanizer, how to keep my feet cool, how to patent my inventions, how to furnish my own den and, most promising of all, how to escape backwoods tedium by sending off and getting lots of mail—a device by which you—damn you—have put me upon several thousand sucker lists.

"I have booklets on how to run a locomotive, how to make a hen coop, how to improve my memory and breed mink. I have received by express the latest information on birth control. I have postcards informing me that in response to my application I will shortly receive on 30-day trial four canoes, six typewriters, one pair of shoe trees, three motorcycles, nine automatic revolvers, one Ostermoor mattress and two invalid chairs. I am as good as matriculated at the Moody Bible Institute and am expecting tomorrow for examination a set of Bob Ingersoll. Just as I left, the mailman brought in a six-foot length of two-inch board and the free book on 'White Pine Value in Home Building.' "

He stamped out, bluing the air as he went. Two days went by and he came in with, "Who may Miss Georgia Wharton be? I have no children. Yet Georgia, at my address, is getting the damnedest response to her inquiries about depilatories, corsets, wrist watches, dude ranches, corn plasters, lady barber colleges, Rhode Island Reds, and correspondence courses in hotel matrons' jobs. She has received twelve samples of perfumes for which there is apparently no dealer in her neighborhood, and a confidential pamphlet teaching her how to administer by stealth the drugs which will rob her father of the liquor habit.

"And, furthermore, just who is Master Georgie Wharton at my address? He seems to have decided that since he is a MANLY Boy ready to be TRAINED FOR LIFE, he would like to see the large illustrated catalogues of some 175 military academies all situated most healthfully in the mountains. He has also sent off for a three-day peek into a book called *Sexology*."

Things went on like this for weeks; then one day George stormed in with, "You've gone too far! As I walked up to my office this morning, a man with a black bag got up from where he had been sitting on the top step and followed me in and said, 'Mr. Wharton, raise

both your arms!' I did, and shut my eyes. A holdup at
last! But the next thing I knew he said, 'You needn't un-
dress; this is just for size,' and he snapped a truss on me.

"He said, 'Your letter stated you ruptured yourself
lifting a cow out of a swamp in 1912—now if you'd
rather, we have it in tan, too.' "

Beyond Flesh and Blood

TO those who sat in the $100 seats at Yankee Stadium the other night, the Joe Louis-Billy Conn ceremonies were apparently quite dull.

But not to me, who sat a thousand miles away, hearing it by radio. What I was seeing was not this droning pursuit of a mouse by a tomcat, but another night altogether, eight years before almost to the day—a night of fog and lightning, fury and awe, fright and drama—June 22, 1938—when Louis had sent Max Schmeling to the floor —and the hospital.

It had been the high-water mark of Joe's life—and, I suspect, mine.

I had to come to the ringside unprepared for what was to happen. For days in Louis' training camp I had heard his handlers murmuring about what Joe was going to do to the German, but I had put all this down as the customary smokeups, the traditional buildups for the sale of seats. To my eye Joe, in his practice quarters, had been the sleepy boy of old, eager to be done with his sparring chores and get back to the ice-cream cones, the apples, and the comic sections which were his delight.

Outwardly he seemed to have no memory of that earlier defeat Schmeling had given him—knocking Joe out for the first time in his career—and to no sport writer had Louis confessed the pain he had felt when Schmeling had gone back to Hitler's Germany in triumph, sneering at Joe, at the Negro race, and at a democracy, such as America, which would allow a black man to become top dog in any field.

Practically a deaf mute anyway in those days, Joe had not made it known that Schmeling's insults had been his first personal contact with race prejudice. From boyhood Joe had been knocking out white boys in amateur rings and had been treated by them as an equal to say the least. The white men's newspapers had trumpeted his fame ever since he had, in his teens, begun to show his incredible power. White men had been proud to talk to him. They had admired his prowess and liked his gentle goodness of character.

Then suddenly he had been, astonishingly, knocked cold, and had heard his conqueror talking about "the master race."

All that, unknown to me, at least, had been gnawing at Joe's soul. Of course, I knew Joe was said to be really training harder than for his first match with Schmeling. At that earlier time Joe had looked upon the German as merely another one of those opponents who kept coming in a long procession to be knocked out in a round or two. Also Joe had been a bridegroom then, and, with his bride in camp, had been surrounded by the mood of roses, singing birds, and dreaming love—a dream from which Schmeling was momentarily to awaken him, then send him to sleep for ten seconds.

But as we sport writers sat at ringside the night of the rematch, I was conscious of no more than that customary tension which comes before the bell at any heavyweight fight. I remember the halo around the white lights, for a fog was rolling up from the river.

Schmeling stood in his corner right above me, waiting with that wave-of-the-future expression on his arrogantly smiling, swarthy face—the expression all Nazis were wearing at the time. Across from him stood Joe, his eyes heavy-lidded, his face impassive as that of a china doll slightly smoked in a backyard bonfire.

The bell rang—and all my life I'll be hearing that sound that came from the ringside—a sharp, sudden, whistling intake of breath from the startled sport writers! Instead of shuffling out slowly as he had always done, his whole body covered with caution, Joe came now in long, rushing strides. Here was a new Joe!

Schmeling confidently swung his right to Joe's jaw—the same blow that had given him victory two years before. But Joe brushed it off and fell like a storm upon the German.

Now the fog that rolled in was suddenly full of red gloves that burst like shells against Schmeling's eyes, his jaws, his lips which almost at once began to drool crimson. He floundered, scrambled, waved his gloves frantically here and there. A sickening right caught him below the left ribs.

I saw it go in. I thought I saw Joe's whole forearm sink in. It made me think of a man reaching in a churn.

It flung Max against the ropes. He clung to them like a seasick passenger to the ship's rail. He leaned on the ropes staring wildly, hopelessly out over a black night sea capped with pandemonium. The ringsiders below him said afterward that, as he hung there, he screamed like a woman in childbirth. On the other side of the platform I couldn't hear that, but I could see enough to scare me. Here was death in the ring. I thought the "Black Death," as Joe was called, had come for the wretched Herr Schmeling.

Here was something beyond flesh and blood. Here was some convulsion of Nature.

Then I saw Joe standing there perfectly still, staring coldly, quiet as the tomb, waiting, waiting for Schmeling to turn around. He made no move to finish it. He couldn't have stood there long, for the whole fight was over in two minutes and four seconds, but it seemed a century to me before Schmeling finally slid along the ropes and then wheeled and tried to face his doom.

The storm broke again and Max smashed to the floor, scrambled up at the count of "two," smashed down again, got up at "one," and then was catapulted down to stay. At the count of "eight," his manager, Max Machon, threw in a towel—it was as white as Machon's face—and crawled through the ropes in surrender. He picked up his mangled man and, with Referee Arthur Donovan helping, dragged him from the ring which was already filling with hysterical people, pawing at Louis. Joe now was jumping up and down, his face glowing probably for the only time, before or since, with the thing called emotion.

Such a night will come no more to Joe, nor, I suspect, to any man, for I had it on the considered word of the skilled and judicial Referee Donovan next day that Louis, that night, could have whipped any man who ever lived.

"How long would Dempsey have lasted against him," I asked.

"No longer than Schmeling," said Donovan. "And John L. Sullivan? Not as long."

Double Martyrdom for Lincoln

CONSIDERING how most Lincoln plays let the theme of sacrifice wreck realism the moment the curtain goes up, I don't know but that I prefer the amateur performance the Cube Experimental Art Theater gave in Chicago on April 12, 1934. It was a performance in which Lincoln was martyred not once but twice.

The amateurs had conceived an original approach to the traditional theme. They reconstructed the scene of Lincoln's murder: revived *Our American Cousin* just as it was played at Ford's Opera House in Washington that fatal night in 1865, and had Mr. Lincoln sitting in the box looking on. Due to the cramped quarters of the hayloft in which they were performing, they had to place the box at one side of the first row of seats, which was not bad since it made Lincoln more one of us than if he had been, as in real life, in a box that was virtually on the stage.

Our American Cousin, as it was performed in costume, proved to be a terrible bore, a dull play about a supposedly witty Yankee who, visiting England, comes it over the earls and ladies with vast ease. Time had mildewed the lines, and Myron Brundage, the amateur actor who was playing Lincoln, wasn't actor enough to laugh at the jibes and jokes as had the President the night he saw it.

Our 1934 Lincoln tried to keep his mind on the play, but its tedium began to get to him along in the middle of Act One and, from my critic's seat, I thought I saw him doze a little now and then. Between acts he tried to shake off boredom by taking a turn in the lobby and sneaking a couple of puffs off pretty Mrs. Lincoln's cigarette— taking good care not to get his whiskers afire.

Back in the theater for Act Two, Lincoln did his best to concentrate on the drowsy business that was transpiring on the stage, but as the evening wore on I caught him looking out of the side of his eyes at the audience and then, when sure it wasn't watching him, openly turning his face to the rear door of the little auditorium. There was appeal in those eyes, as if he were looking for someone, and all at once I realized that he was praying for John Wilkes Booth to come and set him free. He could hardly wait, though he knew his assassination couldn't come till midway of Act Three.

Once, however, I saw an incredulous hope leap into his sad eyes. That came when a loud "Bang" in the back of the house interrupted the actors. Lincoln started to fall lifeless, then caught himself, for it had only been a camp chair collapsing under a heavy patron. Lincoln sagged notably as he returned to the monotony of his own death watch, and he sat in his Presidential box through the next intermission, evidently too weary to stretch his legs.

In the lobby, this intermission I myself brightened somewhat when the imaginative manager of the amateur company, a young man more inventive than learned, told me, "The big climax is coming soon now; John Wyckes Brooks comes right in this back door, you see, slips around back of the audience, goes up to the box and lets Lincoln have it."

I tried to explain to the manager that he had John Wilkes Booth mixed up with Van Wyck Brooks, but he had no time for such hairsplitting in a moment like this.

Back in the theater for Act Three, I saw Lincoln start the session with something like animation in his face. A patient man, he would soon have his reward. But every minute was an hour. The dialogue got duller and duller, and eventually you could see all hope of release dying in his sad eyes.

Then came a whispering in the back of the house and Van Wyck—I mean John Wilkes—Booth in a villain's cloak and black wig, crept up, knelt by the Presidential box and then suddenly arose and pointed a toy pistol at Lincoln's head. Nothing happened. No explosion. Lincoln looked around in disappointment. John Wyckes Booth muttered, "Pshaw," cocked the pistol again and took aim once more.

This time there was only a loud snapping click. But it was good enough for Lincoln, and he fell back in his chair, while his assassin, leaping into the box, wrestled ardently with young Mrs. Lincoln for what seemed to be an unnecessarily long time before condescending to get onto the stage and cry, *"Sic Semper Tyrannis."*

The lights went out and we all went home, feeling it was somehow not quite right to have had an assassination scene in which it sounded as though the villain had got Lincoln in a very large rattrap.

"The Glory-to-God Man"

THE hatters of Troy, jostling other Trojans to read the startling news in the papers, wondered when they saw that the man who had just shot John Wilkes Booth was Sergeant Boston Corbett of the 16th New York Cavalry.

Could that be the same fellow who had worked beside them in Rousseau & Boughton's hat factory before the war?

They read on. It said that the heroic trooper who had avenged the murder of Lincoln had "offered an audible prayer for his victim's soul as he launched him into eternity."

At this, the hatters slapped their thighs and exclaimed, "That's Corbett!" It could have been nobody else.

William Rousseau went around town telling how close he and Corbett had been in the old days: "I taught him to load the first gun he ever fired off." Others recalled the time, eleven years before, when Corbett had dived repeatedly into the icy river to bring up bodies from a ship which had sunk near the docks.

Soon readers everywhere were able to slake their curiosity about the new hero, for the newspapers found hatters who had also worked with him in Albany, in New York, and in Boston. Moreover street evangelists and missionaries in these cities came forward with stories about him. And then there were the interviews which the great man, himself, gave right and left when he rode back with his detachment from Virginia to Washington after their successful chase of Booth.

Reporters usually had to fight through throngs to get at Corbett. One worshiper offered him $1,000 for his revolver with its five unexploded chambers. Corbett wouldn't sell. Photographers dragged at him to get him before their cameras. Quickly his portraits were out-selling Sheridan's.

Day by day the readers got the Great Man's story:

His name had been Thomas P. Corbett when, at the age of seven, he had been brought to America by his English parents in 1839. Either growing up in Troy, or coming there as a hatter's apprentice when young, he was a journeyman in that craft by 1854. "Journeyman" was the word for him. He left Troy for Albany, went to Richmond, Virginia, to New York City, returned to Troy, and then went off again.

It was while working in a New York hattery that he married and met sorrow, his wife dying in childbirth with her tiny daughter already cold beside her. This had driven him to drink, and he had been in Boston, headed downgrade, when one night in 1857 he stopped to listen to street-evangelists and was saved. Under the preacher's words, he saw himself revealed as a sinner and liquor as a gaudy crime. His soul swam up before him as a precious thing, demanding fleshy sacrifice. He marched to the mourners' bench and joined up for life.

Choosing the Methodist Church, he cast about for a Christian name with which to be crowned at baptism. He said that Christ had renamed his disciples when He called them. Corbett settled upon "Boston" as a suitable reward for the city of his rebirth. The "Thomas P." disappeared and Boston Corbett he became.

His life now had a purpose—Reform.

Great days set in. Every evening when the sun was down he struck off, full of supper and glory, to help the street-evangelists with their salvage. But instead of helping, he nearly ruined them. They found it impossible to be heard above his yelping exultations. His ecstatic shouts of "Come to Christ" and "Glory to God" drowned out everything else and, at length, harassed too much by their prize, they blessed him and told him that the time had come for him to carry on alone.

He nearly ruined Samuel Mason, Jr., too—Mason being his employer at the time. Hat-making was a matter of co-ordinating hands with the workmen sitting in long rows, passing hats from hand to hand. All day Corbett had sat in such a line, but after his conversion, nothing could keep him there for long. Whenever one of his comrades dropped an oath or a wish for a drink of liquor, down Boston would go on his knees and up would go Boston's voice in prolonged prayer. Naturally, the hats had to wait. Naturally, too, Samuel Mason, Jr., began to teeter toward the brink of bankruptcy and he did not escape it until he, like the evangelists, had blessed Corbett and let him go.

Eight years later when Corbett was so famous, Mason's daughter looked at his latest photograph and said, "They must have cut his hair in the army, for when he was here, he wore it like Jesus Christ, long and parted in the middle."

Taking the word of his conversion back to Troy, Corbett pleased the State Street Methodist congregation with his zeal but plagued it with his tumult, the Troy *Times* reporting in 1865:

"He gave way to his emotions at prayer meetings and other gatherings and instead of mere 'amens' to denote his feelings, would utter a 'w-h-o-o-p' like an Indian, interrupting, often amazingly, the more quiet members."

Following the current pattern by which a man if he became a reformer in one field became a reformer in all, Corbett added the destruction of slavery to his campaign against sin and rum. He invaded the South in the late 'Fifties, attempting in Richmond, Virginia, to convert the hatters to Jesus and the Chivalry to Abolition. The Southrons quickly chased him back across the Potomac.

Back in the city of Boston, he appeared on the books of the Massachusetts General Hospital as receiving, on July 16 and August 18, 1858, treatments for "self-castration." The explanation was that two street-walkers had ogled him so unbearably one night while he was praying on his soap-box, that he had cried out that his usefulness to the world must not be wrecked by "bad thoughts" and, leaping off his perch, had broken for home where he mutilated himself.

Between the time of his own stroke for personal freedom and the outbreak of the Civil War, Corbett wandered through Eastern cities finishing hats and spending his income on religious tracts which he gave away on the streets. In a hat-factory on Broadway, in New York, he raised objection to his employer's practice of reblocking old hats and selling them at $5. Corbett denounced this as immoral—the hats were worth no more than $3.50— and moved on.

As the South moved closer to Secession, Corbett's wrath

mounted. He produced something like a panic among the ladies of the Attorney Street Methodist Church in New York by declaring in the midst of a religious harangue that he was going to enlist and shoot Southrons on sight!

"I will say to them, 'God have mercy on your souls,' and then pop them off."

One of the first to respond to Lincoln's call for volunteers, he enlisted in the 12th New York regiment of militia on April 12, 1861, but not even the rigorous drilling or the loss of his Messianic haircut could curtail his passion for saving souls. Night and morning, he prayed in his tent, paying no attention to the jeers of the soldiers, who took to calling him "The Glory-To-God Man."

On one of those days of drilling in Franklin Square, New York, when the regimental commander, Colonel Butterfield, was cursing the recruits for awkwardness, Boston Corbett stepped out from the ranks, saluted and asked, in a kind but firm voice, "Colonel, don't you know you are breaking God's law?"

"Take him to the guardhouse!" howled the Colonel.

Incarceration, however, cooled off the Christian martyr not at all, since the baffled Colonel could hear him inside there shouting hymns with joyous fervor. When ordered to stop that racket, Corbett only sang the louder. Finally Butterfield sent him word that he would be liberated if he would apologize for insulting a superior officer.

"No," Boston told the emissary, "I have only offended the colonel, while the colonel has offended God, and I shall never ask the colonel's pardon until he himself has asked pardon of God."

In the face of such determination there was nothing for the colonel to do but turn the prisoner loose, and

Corbett came out smiling with the Good Book under his arm to announce, "I had a good time in there with my God and my Bible."

A problem, indeed, to his superiors, he spent many of those early days in the guardhouse or patrolling a beat with his knapsack full of bricks as punishment for insubordination. While he walked out such sentences, he preached to all who blundered within earshot, warning them against swearing and drinking, and calling upon the wild boys to seek the Lord.

Toward the close of his first enlistment, he announced that his time would be out on a certain midnight, and only smiled when the officers explained that the records showed the date to be several days later. On the chosen midnight he calmly walked off sentry-post and began packing up his things in his tent. Court-martialed, he was sentenced to death for desertion but, according to the stories he told later, he had been spared by President Lincoln to whom Colonel Butterfield got the case referred.

The first day he was free he re-enlisted—this time in the 16th New York Cavalry. As a matter of fact, what with the varying terms of regiments, he had enlisted three times—some said four—by the time the war was done. In spite of everything, colonels were glad to get him, for he was a hell-cat in battle.

Colonel Mosby, the Confederate raider, who was considerable of a hell-cat in battle himself, met Corbett once, and according to Corbett, admired him. It happened in June, 1864, when he was cornered with a squad of men by Mosby in Virginia. Those of his comrades who were not shot down, escaped, leaving no one but the emasculated zealot to face the circling Rebels. For a time he held twenty-six of them at bay. When his ammunition ran out, he made ready to club his foes, and would have been shot down, so he said, if Mosby hadn't struck up the rifles and told his men to bring him the brave fellow alive. Before them all Mosby complimented Corbett— and sent him to the dubious reward of Andersonville Prison.

After the war was over, Corbett told reporters what God had done for him during this portion of his service:

"I faced and fought against a whole column of them, all alone, none but God being with me to help me, my being in a large field and they being in the road with a high board-fence between us enabled me to hold out as long as I did. They finally had the fence down, then closed around me when my pistol gave out, giving me no more fire. I was captured by them and sent to Andersonville, Georgia.

"There God was good to me, sparing my life while another and myself lived out of fourteen men of my own company. But, bless the Lord, a score of souls were converted right on the spot where I lay for three months with no shelter. Many others were converted, for meetings were held in different parts of the 'bull pen.' "

He elaborated on this theme when, on August 28, 1865, in the full glory of his vengeance upon Booth, he was called to the witness stand in the War Department's military trial of Captain Henry Wirz, the loathed head-jailer at Andersonville, that most infamous of prison pens maintained by the Confederacy. With the whole North clamoring for the head of the man whom it believed responsible for the tortures, the insanities, the starvation, the deaths of 10,000 Union soldiers, Wirz was arraigned on an awesome series of charges, the most sensational, though not the most serious, being the claim that he had kept a pack of "ferocious and blood-thirsty beasts, called bloodhounds" which he had "willfully suffered, incited and encouraged to seize, tear, mangle and maim the bodies and limbs" of escaping prisoners. The Government charged that about fifty of these recaptured fugitives had died from dog bites and that those who didn't die were tortured by Wirz for the crime of attempting to run away.

What made the specification about the bloodhounds so important was that it would catch the public eye quicker than the more medical charges about starvation diets, impure vaccines, and unsanitary conditions. There would be popular understanding of the "dead-line," that ill-defined mark some twenty feet inside the stockade over which careless, ignorant, or demented prisoners would sometimes blunder and be shot by sentries. And there would be public wrath if the Government could prove, as it hoped to do, that Wirz had often boasted that he was doing more to damage the Northern armies than if he were leading a Confederate division at the front. But nothing could grip the imagination of the reading world more quickly, here at the outset of the trial, than those baying bloodhounds, for still fresh was the immemorial horror of those hounds chasing Eliza across the ice in *Uncle Tom's Cabin*. Anti-slavery literature as a whole had been dark with savage hounds tearing runaway slaves limb from limb. Tales of fiendish Southerners chasing the Union fugitives from many prison camps had been published during the war. Sherman's men on their devastating sweep through Georgia and the Carolinas had shot hounds wherever they had seen them.

The prosecution, in examining the first seven witnesses, had failed to produce much evidence against Wirz and the dogs before Sergeant Corbett was called to the stand. Three men had testified chiefly about who was who in the case, and two physicians had given a general picture of conditions, bad enough for Wirz, but not linking him to the hounds in damaging fashion. One of the latter, a prisoner who had been a hospital steward before entering Andersonville, testified that he had heard a dying man blame the dogs for his wounds, but the witness couldn't recall the dead man's name. Two enlisted men had, in their testimony, mentioned the dogs not at all.

Then Corbett, the lion of the hour, strode to the stand, the reporters sharpening their pencils. The word went over Washington that the great man was talking.

The hero took his time, for among all his congregations there had never before been one of shoulder-straps. All those long hours on soap-boxes preaching hell-fire to listening street-throngs now stood Boston in good stead. Nothing but Inferno could have rivaled his picture of Andersonville, with four or five of its twenty-six acres "a living mass of putrefaction." A monstrous stench rose from the whole pen, where more than 30,000 men lived in the open under the broiling sun of Georgia, but from a swamp bordering the creek which ran through the stockade, came unnameable odors. "There," said Corbett, "were maggots a foot deep or more," with helpless men lying "in their own filth," wretches who, in the last stages of dysentery or with fly-blown and gangrenous wounds, had become so offensive that their more active comrades had driven them off to this more fecal quarter of the grounds. Moving among these lost men, bringing them the miasmic water from the creek—the only water to be had—Corbett said he had had a good chance to note conditions. He had seen one man die there from lice; when he was stripped as most dead men were by their ragged comrades—lice were seen to cover him "like a garment—a living mass."

Corbett had seen the skeleton-like dead brought out from the miserable hospital and placed in rows like wood ready to be corded. It had horrified him to see prisoners vie for the privilege of carrying the dead to the cemetery outside the stockade, for the reward was permission to bring back firewood which could be sold for a dollar an armload.

"I have often heard those who could not get a chance to carry out a dead man, say to those who did, 'That is right; trade him for good wood!' The prisoners seemed in many cases totally depraved and demoralized. Their minds . . . idiotic."

The food, Corbett continued, was so scanty and so bad that almost everybody had scurvy; his own legs were twisted out of shape for a time, and his gums still bled.

No, he had never seen a man shot at the deadline, but he had heard the sentries' guns going in the night and seen a man whom it was said had just been shot for reaching over the deadline to try and get purer water from the place where the creek flowed in under the stockade.

Corbett swore that he had spent much time warning new prisoners about the brutality of the guards at this imaginary boundary.

He spoke with an almost clerical sadness about a sinful sutler—a prisoner who was permitted to bring in food for resale to his comrades—a man so greedy as to let penniless men starve beside his wagon. No one expected this sutler to bankrupt himself, but "it was his Christian duty to give away a portion of his goods," said Boston.

On most counts Corbett's testimony was satisfyingly horrible to the prosecution, particularly when he summarized, "So great was the horror and misery of that place that I myself had thoughts of going over that deadline to be shot in preference to living there. But it immediately occurred to my mind that it was a Christian's duty to bear whatever was thrown upon me."

It was only when counsel got Corbett eventually onto the dogs that he linked Wirz directly with the crimes.

Boston came to the hounds leisurely, describing how he had told his fellows that he would make a break for freedom at the first opportunity. That had come in October, 1864, when he, with some twenty others, were permitted to go outside for firewood. Watching his chance, he hid and lay there for an hour before he heard the hounds baying on his trail. Nearer and nearer they came, till at last one thrust its wicked muzzle through the brush. Corbett was ready to spring upon the brute, grapple with it and try to throttle it, when a miracle happened!

The bloodhound "rubbed its nose against my face" while the rest of the pack, "instead of tearing me, made a circle and kept running about me until the hunter came." And that fearsome official promptly blew his horn, called the dogs off, spoke "cleverly" and "kindly" to Corbett, and added, "The old man told me to make the dogs tear you, but I have been a prisoner myself and know what it is to be a prisoner and I would not like to do that."

Corbett, warming to his theme, testified, "I believe that the only reason why the hound did not tear me was because the same power kept him from doing it that kept the lions from tearing Daniel—that God in whom I trusted. I believe the Almighty prevented him from biting me."

Boston volunteered the additional information that when the huntsman had brought him to headquarters and Captain Wirz had asked why he hadn't let the dogs tear this man, the man had answered, "I guess the dogs hurt him enough." Wirz hadn't pressed the matter further and had merely ordered the prisoner returned to the stockade. Evidently, Wirz had been moved by something, for he ignored in Corbett's case the usual punishments put upon men for attempting escape.

This was very disappointing to the prosecution; more testimony like this and Wirz would go free. The star witness had produced nothing worse against the bloodhounds than that one of them had kissed him.

The prosecutor let Corbett step down and go away while he himself went at the task of extracting from 140 other witnesses, who would be less colored by religion, such information as would convince the military commission and the outside world that Wirz and the dogs were both guilty and that Wirz should hang—which he eventually did between the hours of 10 and 11 A.M. on November 10, 1865.

It was late in October or early November of 1864 when Corbett was removed from Andersonville to another prison, the evidence failing to show if Captain Wirz had, like all those hatters and preachers in the past, managed to get rid of Boston in self-defense. More likely Corbett was merely one of the many prisoners hastily transferred from Andersonville when Sherman's marchers began to get ready to come down through Georgia toward the sea.

On November 19, 1864, Corbett was exchanged and came North to spend some months in a government hospital at Annapolis, then to enjoy a thirty-day furlough which, though he was still far from well, he spent in labors for the Lord. In February he wrote his pastor: "Do try and lead him [a sinful acquaintance] to Jesus. Brother Irvine is here with me and we often kneel together and besiege the throne of grace and bless God. He makes us happy in His love. We do not forget our pastors and churches and brethren, and we feel that we are not forgotten by those whom we have left for a while. Last night another brother, who belonged to our regiment, had a season of prayer with us reading the Word, and we three were just as happy as in a Big Meeting. Brother Corbett shouted and nobody was hurt by it. Glory to God."

By April he was back at regimental headquarters applying for reinstatement and his papers came just as Lee surrendered.

The regiment was at Vienna, Virginia, twelve miles out of Washington, on Saturday, April 15, when the news came that Lincoln was killed. With other cavalry organizations it was rushed out to search and scout for the fugitive Booth and his silly-boy follower, Davy Herold, who had fled South. Corbett was in the detachment which rode in the procession which took the dead Lincoln to his funeral train.

On Sunday night, April 23, the "glory-to-God man" spoke at McKendree Chapel, a soul-saving center in Washington. He had spoken there before, had, in fact, made a tremendous nuisance of himself with his never-ending bellows, but this visit was remarkable, according to the story he told some days later when celebrity had blessed him. He said that on this night he had prayed with great earnestness to God not to lay innocent blood to the charge of the North, but to bring the guilty to punishment. He had announced that night his assurance that Booth would be delivered into his hands in accord with his prayers.

The next afternoon he was the sergeant of a detachment which volunteered at Major General Hancock's call, to accompany two Secret Service operatives, Colonel Conger and Lieutenant Baker, on a new trail across the Rappahannock River. Now the hunt, which had been for ten days wild and fumbling, began to sharpen. A fresh scent had been disclosed by a Virginia Negro, and at 2 P.M. Corbett and twenty-five troopers under Lieutenant Doherty set out with the detectives. The trail grew hot in the deep night of Tuesday the twenty-fifth, and at two in the morning Booth and Herold were treed in a tobacco barn. The soldiers closed in, mindful of the order that no one was to fire without specific permission, so great was the War Department's wish to take the assassin alive. Lieutenant Doherty found his men so saddle-sore and weary that he assigned each some stick, fence-post, stone or minor landmark to be sure he did not stray away. Sergeant Corbett's place was some thirty feet from the side of the tobacco barn.

There were arguments through the door between Booth and the detectives, some appeals for peaceable surrender from without and some defiances from within. Finally Booth's companion, Herold, emerged with twitters and was bound. When it became apparent that the actor, Booth, preferred to make speeches and engage in heroic dialogue rather than surrender, the detectives fired the barn. Lieutenant Doherty had kept warning them that the thing must be hurried up, Secession sympathizers might rally in force and rescue the assassin.

The flames rose, popping and snapping through the hay on the barn floor. Smoke and flames hid Booth, revealed him, hid him again from eyes pressed to the cracks in the boards. Suddenly a shot cracked above the reports of the burning wood and Booth fell. Lieutenant Baker, who had opened the door a little the better to see, sprang inside and dropped beside the fallen man. Conger came tumbling in, too, shouting, "He shot himself." Baker retorted, "He didn't either. The man who shot him should go back to Washington tonight in irons."

But the man who admitted killing Booth was not only free of irons but very full of triumph as the cavalcade started back for Washington. His lieutenant had not moved to discipline him.

Voices had called from the unseen and their servant had left his post, stepped nearer to the crack, taken careful aim with his revolver resting across his arm, and had shot Booth in the back of the head—a remarkable shot, as he promptly admitted.

Conger, passing Corbett while Booth was being carried out of the blaze, asked, "Why did you fire against orders?"

Boston, preening himself in the glare of the mounting flames, put Conger in his place by citing a higher command.

"God Almighty directed me," he replied, prompting Conger to snap back, "I guess He did, or you could never have hit Booth through that crack in the barn."

Corbett's first official statement about this shot when

he returned to official Washington was that he had "aimed at Booth's body as I did not want to kill him." He had aimed specifically at Booth's shoulder but had hit him just below the right ear. "I think he stooped to pick up something just as I fired. . . . I was afraid if I did not wound him he would kill some of our men."

Later, apparently discovering that he was not to be punished by the War Department for disobedience of orders, he told reporters that God had directed the bullet into the same part of Booth's skull that Booth's bullet had entered Lincoln's. Boston said that he had prayed for Divine guidance as he pressed the trigger, also for Booth's soul: "I always make such prayers when shooting rebels," he said.

He was, nevertheless, careful when testifying at the trial of the Lincoln conspirators, to state that he had fired at Booth when the latter raised his carbine, aiming "at whom I could not say." He added, "My mind was upon him attentively to see that he did no harm, and, when I became impressed that it was time, I shot him."

Not only did the newspapers rejoice that the sergeant was exempted from punishment, they attacked the War Department for not promoting him, and some of them were outraged when, in the division of the reward that had been offered for the apprehension of Booth and Herold, Corbett received no more than the private soldiers—a share amounting to $1,653.85—while the commissioned officers and detectives received larger sums.

Corbett was bland about this furor, saying that he wished nothing special for having done what God told him to do. He told a New York *Tribune* man, however, that if the Government wished to reward him and would allow him to keep his little saddle horse when his term of service was over, it would be all he could wish. He wasn't very valuable, but "I've got so attached to him that I would like to take him home."

Although there is no record of his wish being granted, Corbett did receive from Lieutenant Doherty when his muster-out papers came on August 17, 1865, the compliment that "in military capacity he is second to none in the service."

Back in civil life again, Boston took to the lecture platform. Churches, ladies' clubs, Sunday schools, religious leagues, patriotic bodies, temperance units besought him to address them. But they never besought him a second time. His lectures turned into wild incoherencies on religion, and, before long, the patriots and even the churchfolk found their curiosity degenerating into yawns.

Soon he was back finishing hats again in the shop of his former employer, Samuel Mason, Jr., who now looked upon his once-troublesome worker with patriotic eye. This job failed, too, a little later when the style in men's headgear changed, throwing the hat-finishers out of work. Corbett, returning to soul salvation, became lay-preacher for a poor congregation of Methodist Episcopalians at Camden, New Jersey. Here he lasted a few months before his flock blessed him and shoved him on.

Rattling around the East for a time, he disappeared from public view.

One day he popped into the Judge-Advocate office in the War Department at Washington, asking to see the souvenirs of Lincoln's assassination preserved there. John P. Simington, the clerk in charge, showed him Booth's boot and pistol, also Boston's own revolver which he had handed in when mustered out of service. It still had five of its six chambers full. Booth's pistol was loaded, too, and when Corbett grabbed both weapons and started ranting, the office was in terror.

"He ran past my desk," said Simington, years later, "and all over the place, waving those pistols. He was crazy. You could tell it by looking at his face. I was certainly glad when we finally got those guns away from him."

It was as a mad hatter that Corbett was known, by such as did know him, when in 1878 he quit the East and went homesteading to Kansas as so many Union veterans had done. Farming, near Concordia, was, however, too slow for one who had known the rush of fame, and Corbett was soon laboring in the vineyard of the Lord rather than on his own acres, preaching up and down the countryside.

For the Kansans he worked up his most ambitious lecture, one with magic lantern slides of Booth, of himself before he shot Booth and after he shot Booth, slides of Lincoln and Tad, slides of the four conspirators hanging by their necks. This show of his had some success at first, then the old story—the lecture turning into loud shouts about the glory of God, audiences eventually nodding in their seats or stamping out to untie their horses and be off for home across the Kansas night-roads. The farmers, too, blessed him and shoved him on.

In the next decade Corbett was a wanderer, preaching, canvassing, fiddling about, trifling with great energy. Some time in 1886 the Grand Army of the Republic obtained for him the post of doorkeeper of the Kansas State Legislature. For a time this honor sufficed, then on the morning of February 15, 1887, he quietly locked the

doors on the State Representatives, and drew forth two
large revolvers. In his best evangelistic voice he informed
the members that God demanded their lives, and cut loose
with both guns.

Jehovah, however, did not direct these bullets as well
for him as He had done on that Virginia night twenty
years before, and Corbett hit none of the frenzied solons
who tore about the room, hiding behind desks and waste-
paper baskets, trying to claw their way up smooth walls
into the balcony or butting wildly into the locked doors.

Eventually pacified, Corbett felt the lawmakers patting
him on the back for services to the flag, heard them wish
him well—and he was shoved on again—this time into the
Kansas asylum for the insane at Topeka.

Stone walls had never a prison been to Corbett and the
man who had tried to break out of Andersonville could
not reasonably expect to rot in an ordinary madhouse.
A year and a half after his entrance, he was written off the
asylum's books as "escaped."

On May 26, 1888, Corbett with other inmates had
been marching along a road in the grounds when a boy
had ridden up, tied his horse and wandered off sightseeing
around the institution. As the men filed past the horse,
Corbett scrambled into the saddle and was off. A week
later he was at Neodesha on this horse, telling an old
companion from Andersonville days of the shameful treatment the nation had given him. As he left, he said he was
going to Mexico.

This was the last his legal guardian, Judge Huron of
Topeka, ever heard of him, although in 1905, it was
thought he had been discovered in Dallas, Texas. It was
only an impostor, however, and nothing more was heard

of the mad hatter until Osborn H. Oldroyd, a collector of Lincolniana, in 1901 declared he had located him "at the age of sixty-two," selling patent medicine over Oklahoma and Texas, with headquarters at Enid, in the former state. While other students of Lincolniana knew that Oldroyd was mistaken as to Corbett's age, the evidence of Corbett's residence at Enid might have been more accurate.

Enid, curiously enough, was the very town, of all small towns in the Southwest, where lived a mysterious house-painter, David E. George, alias John St. Helen, who in mid-April, 1902, fearing that he was dying, confessed that he was really John Wilkes Booth, who had escaped after killing Lincoln, and had left some other man to be shot in his place. Recovering, as an uncomfortable anti-climax, the bibulous house-painter was testy about the confession, and his confidants concealed the matter for a time, if, indeed, they ever gave it any credence. It was not until after January 14, 1903, when, dying by suicide, he made his gaudy confession anew to bedside listeners, that the story gained circulation.

If Corbett was still living when this hoax commanded so much credence in Oklahoma, it must have been a shock to him to have his famous deed so discounted. Probably Boston was dead at the time, but even if alive, he would have been seventy-one, too old to have put up much of a fight against the story as repeated by the credulous Southwesterners.

One can only speculate upon his end. Myth-makers are welcome to play with it. How satisfying to them to describe Corbett, an old, old man, meeting his supposed victim of two-score years before—meeting John Wilkes

Booth on the streets of Enid, Oklahoma, and falling dead from the shock, even as he reached for his gun to shoot his man again.

More likely Corbett went to glory in some Oklahoma drugstore, stricken suddenly as, leaning over his patent medicine satchel, he pinned some gaping clerk to the counter with windy threats of that righteous and awful vengeance that is to come.

Sources

(*Note:* The following list is appended for those readers who may want to know the time and place of original publication of the pieces in this book. The sources of the Tom Blevins' pieces, "A Dreamlike Concern" and "Billy the Kid," appear on pages 67 and 101 respectively; the opening selection, "Old Tom's Cabins," was written from many notes made between 1919 and 1930.)

He Hated Southern Gentlemen, *American Mercury*, December, 1929

The Secret Evangel of Otto McFeely, *Chicago Sun*, July 15, 1945

That Cold, Hard Eye, *Chicago Daily News*, May 9, 1936

My Biggest Baseball Day, *Chicago Daily News*, January 23, 1943

The Battle of Kilpatrick's Pants, *American Mercury*, August, 1930 (in which it was published under the title "Taps for the Cavalry")

Last of the Troubadours, *The Chicagoan*, August 17, 1929

The Holy Spirit at West Point, *American Mercury*, November, 1930

The Rats and Cats at Terre Haute, *Chicago Daily News*, June 29, 1932

A Hymn from an Abattoir, *American Mercury*, October, 1931

The Old Judge, *Chicago Daily News*, May 18, 1934

The Hill Called Crowder's Curse, *Chicago Daily News*, October 7, 1935

The Man the Historians Forgot, *Kansas Historical Quarterly*, February, 1939

"Keep Movin'," *Chicago Daily News*, September 20-21, 1940

"De Lawd's" Only Friend, *Chicago Daily News*, February 18, 1932

They Didn't Want "Free Enterprise," *Chicago Sun*, June 24, 1945

Not in "The Green Pastures," *Chicago Sun*, July 29, 1945

King of the Bull Pen, *Chicago Sun*, August 5, 1945

They Are Wrong About Wright, *Chicago Sun*, August 19, 1945

Heave-ho, Silver!, *Chicago Sun*, August 26, 1945

The Great Winnetka Hunt, *Chicago Sun*, September 2, 1945

Reform Is Where You Find It, *Chicago Sun*, September 30, 1945

A Founding Father Returns, *Chicago Sun*, December 9, 1945

The Big Shoulders Sag, *Chicago Sun*, January 20, 1946

Orchids to Mrs. Einstein, *Chicago Sun*, March 10, 1946

Woollcott, Horner & White, *Chicago Sun*, March 24, 1946

Life with Uncle Eggs, *Chicago Sun*, April 21, 28, 1946

Backwoods Aristocrat, *Chicago Sun*, May 26, 1946

"Send Off, and Get Lots of Mail," *Chicago Sun*, June 23, 1946

Beyond Flesh and Blood, *Chicago Sun*, June 30, 1946

Double Martyrdom for Lincoln, *Chicago Sun*, July 21, 1946

"The Glory-to-God Man," expanded, on the basis of new material found in October, 1946, from an article originally published in *Century Magazine*, August, 1928, and included in *Myths After Lincoln*, Harcourt, Brace and Company, 1932